GROWING

UP IN

THE 1950s

Chris Walker

ChrisWalker1812@gmail.com

Also by Chris Walker

Young Love in Sixties Bristol

ISBN 9798613825431

CONTENTS

1

WHAT'S IT ALL ABOUT?

A time long ago, I was a young boy living and learning throughout the 1950s. I am old now but on good days I don't always *feel* as old as the miles on the clock. Which can be quite encouraging. And helpful, when I am putting my mind to remembering my life all those years ago.

In this short book I describe highlights and low-lights of my time at primary and secondary school. No middle school in my day, just primary education for 5- to 10-year-olds, then secondary for 11- to 15-year-olds (extended to 16-year-olds in 1972 after several years in the planning).

Students now, of course, have to remain in some form of further education until they are 18 years old. I was happy to leave school as a 16-year-old, keen to look beyond school and get a job.

I also cover in the forthcoming chapters incidents in my young life outside school, of which I have both fond, and embarrassing, memories. This is a personal account of my life throughout the 1950s; not all events will be in strict chronological order.

In addition to my own experiences, I have tried to give a flavour of living in the 1950s. Later in the book I include references to national and international events that made an impact on me.

My school days were many moons ago, yet I recollect so much. Some reminders of those days have come from intermittent schoolboy diaries I maintained. Deciphering my pencil scrawl has required some effort, including remembering and translating the code I invented for certain activities and very personal thoughts described therein, the code being used as my protection, should the diaries be found by my parents.

The general content of those diaries? Apart from those personal thoughts, most comments related to the amount of homework set, the weather, any specific highlights from the school day (rare), occasionally what we ate for supper and finally the time I retired to my bed; not exactly dynamic, riveting material.

The diaries do give some insight into how I felt from day to day: I was not always a happy and cheerful schoolboy. I have the good fortune to be blessed with a good memory of the 1950s, and the 1960s come to that. The grey matter has been trawled in some depth to source the ensuing pages.

I passed my GCE (now GCSE) English exam and a few others, way back in 1961, so please excuse grammatical errors in the forthcoming chapters. I tend to employ a colloquial writing style rather than scholarly, which might not appeal to the more academic reader. I don't use many long words.

I have been known to mix my tenses and have at times done so in this book; grammatically incorrect I know but this happens if a memory is particularly clear in my mind when composing the sentence. It's a personal thing. To me, it better describes the occasion or event. I have tried to avoid tautology – unlike a colleague of my father who, when asked for his opinion on a matter, invariably started with: 'Well, me myself personally....'

I have probably used too many Oxford commas (one coming up) for some peoples' liking, and you might also spot my sporadic sentence without a verb. I also ask you to please excuse the occasional spelling mitsake. Further, I know I shouldn't use a preposition to end a sentence with. And my English schoolmaster told me it was very wrong to start a sentence with 'And.'

My introduction to the joys of school happened in September 1950, aged 5¼ years, nursery school still rare, and 'rising fives' not known as an expression or category until much later. This special day in my life did not concern me, I was just intrigued as to what it was all about.

I enjoyed good days at school, some less so, benefiting from several original life experiences. But in all honesty, one of the best days of my schooling was the day I left in December 1961, to start a new life, a new exciting life, with fresh opportunities and challenges. Not everyone believes your school days are the best days of your life. But as I said, there were good days…

The book is an account of my personal experiences of growing up in 1950s. My recollections might rekindle in others their own memories of the time. Should there be a reader out there who finds my book of interest, I would be delighted. But one reason for writing about my life in the 1950s is, if I live long enough to have serious memory problems, to then perhaps read the book and maybe say to myself:

'Ah, yes, I remember that.'

2

BEFORE MY SCHOOL DAYS

Not surprisingly, recollection of my *pre*-school years is patchy. My earliest memory is of a vivid event around my third birthday.

My parents reached agreement with a religious orphanage in Stoke Bishop, Bristol, to adopt a 6-month-old girl. On the arranged day we drove along the tree-lined drive to the orphanage, parked the car, and were shown into the nursery. The nun took my parents to the appropriate cot, placing the girl in my mothers' arms.

Susan was to become my sister.

During this emotional event, I noticed a baby in a cot in the far corner of the nursery, crying uncontrollably. The nun noticed me staring:

'He's blind, you know,' the nun whispered. No, I didn't know.

When around 4-years-old, I have a surprisingly clear memory of a holiday on a camping site mid-way between Bridport and West Bay in Dorset. We stayed in a rented static caravan with no indoor facilities apart from the beds, a simple table and bench. Ablutions were carried out in the open-air using a washing bowl supported within a wooden trestle Dad had brought back from his army days in India. Meals were cooked outside the caravan on a gas ring – on reflection, this might even have been a double ring, camping luxury.

We walked to West Bay to stroll on the sand and shingle, and paddle in the sea. Much too cold for swimming, in any case I had not yet learnt how to swim. One evening, we drove into Bridport where Mum and Dad found a pub, allowing plenty of time for the rest of us to study, from the back seat of the car, the comings and goings in the pub car park. I hope our parents kept an eye on us.

I revisited the area recently to see if I could discover where the camp site might have been. Not a chance – this once beautiful part of the Dorset countryside is now an urban sprawl all the way from Bridport to West Bay.

When very young, thunderstorms petrified me. An early memory is of a family picnic: suddenly thunder roared. I crawled under a picnic chair, shrieking in fright. The family laughed, offering me no sympathy nor comfort, clearly relishing the incident. I didn't enjoy that one bit, neither the thunderstorm nor the lack of concern from my parents.

One event I don't remember was a fireside accident, also when about four-years-old. I have been told that on one cold winter afternoon I was playing with my toys in front of the open fire. I watched Dad stoke the fire with the poker whereupon, perhaps unwisely, he left the room. I guess the poker looked like it might be fun to play with so naturally, I picked it up. It was later surmised that the poker was heavier than I expected. It fell on the back of my left hand – I have the remnants of the scar today. A fireguard was hastily installed.

Mother told me years later I could never be a successful criminal with such an identifying mark.

Mention of a fireguard reminds me of occasional visits to my maternal grandfather in Bristol. He suffered from a perpetual cold, unusual for an old man, quite normal for me. He showed me how to deal with a handkerchief, once well-used and moist. He draped the wet hanky on the fireguard and, when dry, put it back in his trouser pocket for future use. He didn't tell me how many times he repeated this imaginative technique with the long-suffering handkerchief. Although not to be recommended, this procedure would have been more economical than using box loads of paper tissues (had they been invented) but rather less hygienic.

On the subject of paper products, soft toilet tissue was unheard of. Well I remember the shiny non-absorbent Izal loo paper, single sheets in a cardboard box, carrying the slogan *Medicated with Izal Germicide.* Gross or what, old newspapers were far more comfortable. Those were bad days for bums.

We kept chickens. These provided us with farm-fresh eggs and the main ingredient for our Sunday roast dinner. Just one problem – Dad couldn't bring himself to wring the neck of the unfortunate selected chicken and had no choice but to ask the milkman to carry out the evil deed. I watched: he seemed to enjoy it.

One day, minding my own business wandering past the chicken run, I was shocked to see a large (to me) rat eating the chicken feed. I ran to Dad, shaking in fear. (All in all, I wasn't the bravest little boy, but to be fair I hadn't yet reached my fifth birthday).

This time, Dad showed paternal concern but quizzed me as to whether it might not have been just a very large mouse. He decided to take no chances though. A rat-catching cage was purchased, poison not being a viable option in view of the chickens. Gingerly, and from a distance, I watched the cage. We never did catch the rat.

3

PRIMARY SCHOOL

My first day

A boy, crying his eyes out.

'What's the matter with him?' I ask.

'He's missing his mummy.'

I hadn't thought about that, hadn't crossed my mind. No time for me to consider whether I might be missing *my* mummy as we were introduced to our first lesson – how to write our name.

I took some time learning to write mine, not easy being known then not as Chris, but Christopher, a challenging long name. Another boy, tall with thick black hair, quite unlike me in stature and appearance, was Joe Mann. I envied that name, so short! I want that name. In all seriousness I asked:

'Joe, will you swop names with me?' He declined.

I was sent to school each day with a clean handkerchief, invariably well and truly grubby by the end of the day. In addition to my clean hanky, my mother also insisted I wore a clean pair of underpants to school. I believed this to be a bit unnecessary but Mum told me why:

'It's in case you have an accident, like getting run over and taken to hospital, we would be mortified if your undies weren't clean.'

Nice set of priorities, I thought. If I was run over my pants were not going to be very clean anyway. I didn't bother to argue.

The First Term

Three days a week the morning started with Assembly. The teaching staff lined up on the stage, the headmaster introduced the service with prayers which we follow with a rousing hymn. Our favourite hymn was *He who would valiant be,* as the more daring among us sung the last line of each verse as '…to be a penguin.' Anarchic or what.

A very relaxed first term with I imagine little academic learning, being broken into this aspect of school gently. The last hour of the school day became much anticipated as 'teacher' read to us,

Enid Blyton's *The Famous Five* and similar. We were encouraged to bring a book from home for this purpose – perhaps for the school to discover which homes actually possessed any books?

I do remember my teachers at primary school, especially Mr Bushell, a fatherly figure, Miss Pullin, petite and forever smiling, and Mr Chown, a very English gentleman although this is not obvious from his name. All the teaching staff were kind and easy-going (unlike secondary school). On my last day of primary education, I collected autographs from all the staff; I still have the book.

A memory of Mr Bushell – I became quite smitten with him, in a way. One early day during this first term I wrapped my arms around his legs (he was a tall man) declaring:

'I love you, Mr Bushell!'

He smiled and walked away. Embarrassing for him and, looking back, embarrassing for me.

My eyesight

During playground chat, I learnt the name of the headmaster, or at least was told it was Mr Marigold. Early on, my father needed to have a word with him to let him know about my poor eyesight and to enquire if I could be seated at the front of the class. Dad asked me for the head's name and duly made an appointment at the school. He later told me I had given him incorrect information as his name was in fact Mr Marriot, not Marigold. I was naïve, easily taken in by inaccurate playground chat.

My eyesight has always been poor. Before receiving my first pair of glasses, just six-years-old, I read the (pre-European standard) road sign 'Major Road Ahead' as 'Mr Joe's Road Ahead'. I misinterpreted several public signs and notices, a few surprises coming my way once adorned with spectacles.

I was, understandably, a little self-conscious – and embarrassed – on my first day at school wearing my new NHS specs. Stylish they were not, but my school friends were nice about it at morning break and I soon became used to my new appearance. The boys at secondary school were not so kind, calling me 'four eyes' and worse on many an occasion.

Break time

Morning break brought the dubious pleasure of our one-third-pint of full cream milk, to my taste pretty sickly, particularly in the summer months when by break time it could be quite warm, occasionally 'on the turn'. Some girls did not drink their allowance but there were invariably others, habitually boys, who ably consumed two or more bottles. Not for me, though, which might explain at least in part why a lack of calcium in my diet led later to possessing a poor set of teeth.

Our primary school language was, not surprisingly, infantile and great amusement could be enjoyed with toilet humour. One break time we held a group discussion in a hidden (we thought) corner of the playground, thinking up the best name for our little attachment. This chat was limited to the boys, girls not invited, although they may have been happy to contribute some interesting suggestions of their own. Philip, a close friend (of whom more later) won the competition with 'tiddler'. Apt, I suppose, bearing in mind our tender age and under-developed body parts.

As I said, the girls were excluded from this survey (who knows what they talked about among themselves) and the boys were excluded from the girls' popular activity – skipping, particularly group relay skipping, which is played as follows:

Two girls swing a skipping rope between them. As a girl skips in, they sing (to the tune of the chorus in Ally's Tartan Army) -

Vote, vote, vote for (e.g.) Emily Braithwaite
Here comes (e.g.) Shirley at the door
Shirley is the one who is having all the fun
So we don't want Emily Braithwaite anymore
Two, four, shut the door!

Emily skips out, Shirley skips in, and so on.

There are regional variations on basically the same song. When not skipping, the girls might just sing from a wide repertoire, a popular song amongst many being *The Big Ship Sails on the Alley-Alley-Oh*.

Dinner Time

At lunchtime, or dinner time as it has always been known in school parlance, we walked, crocodile style, to the school dinner canteen 300 yards up the road at the council recreation ground. We held hands, boy with boy, girl with girl, never boy with girl, at that age not being into that sort of thing. We were not going to volunteer to hold the hand of a girl. Girls were not the same as us. We were aware of a physical difference, not just 'down there', but in their general behaviour and demeanour. Sugar and spice and all things nice? We thought not.

So to dinner, a highlight of the school day for most of us although looking back, the food was never that appetising. I remember boiled potatoes and over-cooked cabbage regularly being served, together with suspicious-looking stews. Not at all enticing but probably healthy. Puddings were noticeably better, especially chocolate fudge served with runny custard, a firm favourite with us all. Other days, rice pudding, semolina or tapioca (frogspawn) appeared on the single-choice menu. I was happy with all of it, though the offerings were not universally liked.

Each Monday morning, we handed over our dinner money. That is, apart from any boys or girls entitled to free school dinners, clearly identified as such in class which must have been an embarrassment for them. It certainly made me feel awkward. In spite of my tender years, I was already to some extent aware of the feelings of other children. On the first such Monday, the teacher asked us to go up to him with our money, but first called out:

'Not you, *(boys' name)*, you get free dinners.'

At break, we asked him why.

'I don't know,' he replied, looking most uncomfortable. Surely a better arrangement should have been in place?

Some of us were allowed home at lunchtime, not me as I lived too far away. In any case, I am pretty sure my mother would not be best pleased with such an interruption to her day, and being required to prepare me a meal.

About the boy/girl thing: sitting in class was a different matter to the walk to dinner as we boys, particularly the troublesome ones, were often placed on a dual desk with a girl. One term, teacher placed me next to Carol Williams, a very pretty girl, popular in class, but I never spoke to her and she never spoke to me.

Listen with Mother

At a quarter to two on weekdays on the Light Programme (now BBC Radio 2) a 15-minute transmission, *Listen with Mother,* was broadcast for mothers at home listening with their under-fives. That's as may be, but I never listened to the programme with my mother. But I do remember the presenter opened the programme with these memorable words:

'Are you sitting comfortably? Then I'll begin.'

I mention the programme as background to one Saturday in December 1951, now in my second year at school, the day of the annual church Christmas bazaar in Melksham, Wiltshire. The event was opened by none other than Daphne Oxenford, the regular presenter of *Listen with Mother.* I have no idea why, but I was chosen to sit on Mrs Oxenford's knee for a photo to be taken by the *Wiltshire Gazette*, the photo being published the following Monday – my first appearance in the media. Trivia alert – Daphne later found further fame as an original cast member on the soap opera *Coronation Street.*

In later years, when families were buying their first television set (of more later), *Watch with Mother* became a popular early TV programme for littles, introducing us to *Andy Pandy*, *Muffin the Mule* and *The Flower Pot Men.*

21

Shortly after the Christmas bazaar and following my appearance in the press, my mother dragged me to the town centre to sing carols with a group of parishioners in front of an audience of local townsfolk, shoppers and the mildly interested.

'Come on, Christopher, move to the front where people can see you'.

I was *so* embarrassed.

Goodbye tonsils

When 6-years-old, I was booked into Melksham cottage hospital to have my tonsils removed, a common procedure at the time as an alleged cure for recurrent infections. I stayed in for the night following the operation and must have looked very bored because a kindly nurse suggested I listen to the wireless. She fitted me with earphones, switched on then promptly left the ward.

I was forgotten by the nurse, presumably also by matron. I didn't know how to remove the headphones and wondered whether *Listen with Mother* would be broadcast again in the middle of the night, at the same hour as the daytime programme. A strange thought but I was still young. I eventually fell asleep.

I woke in the morning, earphones removed during the night, to be greeted with a breakfast of jelly and ice cream. I was very happy with that.

For many years Mum worked part-time at the hospital as an auxiliary nurse and no doubt kept an eye on me if my hospital stay coincided with her shift. I don't remember. Or she might have been otherwise employed at the time, on duty with St. John Ambulance where she worked as a volunteer.

Back to School

Primary school allowed plenty of time for play. Among other activities, we amused ourselves playing marbles and a lively market developed in bartering marbles, comics and various games. A favourite pastime was to cut channels in the sloping turfed area surrounding the school buildings and hold marble races, such fun. The activity was suspended when the groundsman discovered the damage caused to his manicured lawns. He was not happy.

Adjoining the school grounds stood a rambling house with a large garden. This would have been of no interest to us were it not for the golden retriever living there. We loved going up to the hedge to talk to Bella, she was always pleased to see us even though we possessed no food to offer her. She lived in hope.

The school was Lowbourne Primary School in Melksham and is still there. The original building, which I remember well, is unchanged, although new classrooms have been erected in the grounds, albeit with the loss of amenity areas including the grassed area where we played marbles.

Sporadically we talked about our parents. It seemed to us that everyone, boys and girls alike, came from what is called today 'a stable background' with both a mum and a dad at home, unlike the many single-parent families today. Or perhaps our fellow pupils not so blessed just kept quiet.

We were examined regularly for head lice and nits. Do children still go through this indignity? In addition to that, a chiropodist called to check for flat feet. I was never found to be the bearer of head lice, nor nits, but more than once I was given a note to take home, confirming I was suffering from flat feet. I didn't think I was suffering and anyway, my mother always ignored the notes.

We were expected to catch measles, mumps and the rest in the natural way. Any delay in catching these diseases meant an introduction to a child who was so suffering. This was well before the introduction of the MMR vaccine.

A trip to the sweet shop

On the road between the school and town centre stood a traditional sweet shop. We were allowed to visit this delectable store during our lunch hour, provided we obtained permission. We were regulars there. After downing our food, one of us might pipe up:

'Sweet shop, if per poss?' (i.e. if permission possible). One day, permission duly obtained, I accompanied Peter to the shop. Peter Cornish was a fair-haired intelligent boy but with an inability to spell even the simplest of words. He might well have been dyslexic, but we would not have been aware of that expression at the time.

On the day, with no money of my own, I justifiably assumed he would give me a sweet for accompanying him. I pestered him:

'Come on, Pete.'

'No.'

'Give me a sweet, come on, now or never.'

Why did I foolishly say that? He took me at my word, giving his final comment, with a laugh, saying:

'Alright then, never.'

A primary school joke:

Teacher: 'Johnny, if you had six apples and I asked you for one, how many would you have left?'

Johnny: 'Six.'

Walking to school

In my second year at primary school I was allowed – indeed encouraged by my parents – to walk to and from school, the quickest way being by way of the council estate of prefabs (more on prefabricated buildings in a later chapter). My father, for reasons of his own, told me not to walk that way but to walk via the town centre. Which I did.

The plus side of this detour and longer route to school gave me the opportunity on my way home to stop off at the local cake shop to buy an end-of-day stale cake (or two) for one old penny (½p) each. I was always hungry.

Walking through town I regularly saw the Rag and Bone man, but unsure as to what he collected. Surely not just rags and bones? I later learned he gave a few coppers for anything he felt he might resell for a profit. An original Steptoe.

Another regular in town was the ice-cream man on his bicycle with his 'Stop Me and Buy One' sign, crudely misquoted by many a coarse schoolboy as 'Buy Me and Stop One'. Only later did I understand what this misquote meant, being educated by my peers about condoms and what they were used for.

Also on my travels between home and school, I passed the ambulance station. Superstitiously I performed the actions, mumbling the oft-recited words to myself:

Touch my nose, touch my toes, never go in one of those.

There are regional variations of the words.

On Wednesday afternoons I walked past the PDSA van (Peoples Dispensary for Sick Animals) who provided free or reduced-cost veterinary care for small animals. They still do. I remembered my parents complaining about expensive bills from their vet, so I mentioned the PDSA to Dad:

'That's only for poor people, Christopher.'

'But Dad, we are poor!'

He wasn't having any of it.

Some days on my walk to school I could be lost in my thoughts, thinking of the day ahead or more likely of what entertainment I might plan for myself that evening. It was on one such morning, crossing the road in Melksham town centre, correctly using the pedestrian crossing between the Post Office and WH Smith's, I was hit and knocked over by an elderly lady on her bicycle. It was my right-of-way but I received the blame. I continued to school but looked over my shoulder to see the lady being comforted by passers-by. No such comfort for me.

We were warned about talking to strangers. As I was walking home one fine afternoon, a car pulled up alongside me and an elderly gentleman, well to me he looked elderly, offered me a lift home. I stood on the pavement, speechless.

'It's alright', he said, speaking softly and with a smile. 'I'm a school inspector.'

I slowly shook my head and walked on. At the time I thought I was being a bit rude, but on reflection doubted a school inspector would behave in such a manner. I mentioned the incident to my parents but am unaware whether the episode was taken any further.

Arriving home from school I always looked forward to a glass of squash and a sandwich waiting for me on the kitchen table. (I would have polished-off the cake(s) on the one-mile walk home). Our favourite bread was 'Mother's Pride', (a soft white *sliced* bread, a new concept to us). One afternoon, horror of horrors, the breadbin was empty.

'Chrissy, be a love, pop into town, get a Mother's Pride would you, here's the money.'

So, one mile back into town, walking and running to Webster's bakery, a popular family-run store. I arrived at the bakers.

'Can I have a large Mother's Pride, please?'

'Sorry, we only have Webster's Pride here,' the assistant said, with a smirk to his colleague.

I walked home, empty-handed, to be ticked-off. Well, Mum did say 'Mother's Pride', she didn't say buy any old bread. No sandwich for me that afternoon.

Saturday pictures

My parents, perfectly happy for me to walk to school on my own and home again every weekday, yet did not allow me to walk into town on a Saturday to meet up with my school friends for Saturday morning pictures at the local cinema. I still feel a little disgruntled and cheated about missing out on that particular element of my youth but Dad was very firm on the issue, leaving no question of doubt:

'No, Christopher, it would not be appropriate for you to go there, end of.'

Well, he wouldn't have said 'end of' in those days but the message was clear. I think he was worried about the company I might keep, ignoring the fact that some of those attending the cinema were the same boys and girls I mixed with in my class at school.

After the pictures, more commonly known to us as 'the flicks', some of my classmates called in at the milk bar opposite the cinema, but again thanks to Dad this was another significant activity not open to me. Milk bars were popular in the Fifties, later being known as expresso bars, now coffee shops.

An escape

One boy in my class, Eric, suffered an unhappy childhood for which his parents were allegedly responsible. He told me, Peter and Philip, he had decided to run away from home. Yes, we thought, Drama Queen. But he did not return home that night. We were all quizzed by the school and later by the police (dressed in plain clothes). Only later did we discover they were, in fact, the long arm of the law. We hadn't believed Eric meant what he said, not having confided in us how he was planning his escape.

They found him later the next day hiding in a goods wagon at the local railway station, shivering and hungry. He left school shortly after this incident and nothing further was heard of him.

Extramural activities

During my final primary year, I was allocated a small part in the annual school play. One of the teachers was dressed up as royalty, my task being to walk behind her as a page, carrying a decorated paper crown resting on a cushion. Shortly after the play began the crown started to fall apart. Must be my fault, what a mess I've made of my first drama performance, I'm in real trouble. With one hand I carried the cushion, the other hand struggling to hold the crown together.

I had no idea what the play was all about.

That was not my only experience of school drama: I was to suffer a further embarrassing experience at secondary school.

In my final primary school term, a Mayday festival took place, to which parents were invited. The centrepiece of the traditional festival is, of course, the maypole. I was considered too clumsy to be one of the dancers so instead was allocated the task, with two other boys, to hold the maypole steady. I am still quite clumsy to this day, to which others may well attest.

Time to move on

My primary years were ending. This was the era of the Eleven-Plus examination which defined our secondary education route, indeed often decided the life to which most of us were to be destined, and at such a tender young age. This potentially life-changing event was well before the introduction of comprehensive education.

My parents bribed me.

'Christopher, if you pass the tests, we will buy you a watch of your very own.'

They appeared more anxious than me about the exams, being uncharacteristically pleasant and kind.

On the big day, Dad brought me an early morning cup of tea, an unheard-of experience.

Disaster struck. On entering my bedroom, he stepped on my glasses; I always left them on the floor next to my bed. No way was I going to read the exam questions without my glasses. Dad glued the frame and lenses together as best he could and accompanied me to school. He intended to ask the headmaster whether a note might be placed with my examination papers, explaining the circumstances. I have no idea whether this happened.

Despite this domestic catastrophe, I was fortunately successful with the tests, becoming the delighted owner of my first watch, bought from Cleverley's of Melksham for the grand price of £2.10/- (£2.50), no small sum in 1956. I remember being more excited by the watch than by passing the exams.

Now I was eligible to move up to a grammar school – subject to interview. After an anxious wait lasting what seemed like weeks, but probably wasn't, the day of the interview dawned: the day to decide my secondary education. I was worried.

'What if they ask me what I want to do when I grow up?' I asked my father.

'Tell 'em you want to be a doctor.'

That sounds good, I'll use that.

The interview

The interview started well. The interrogators, the headmaster and his deputy, both displayed a kindly, smiling approach. I'm in, I thought. I answered their questions, starting to wonder why I had been so worried.

'Have you read any books?'

'Yes, I like reading Enid Blyton,' I replied, pleased with my quick response. I became quite animated and continued:

'I like all the Adventure books, Famous Five, Secret Seven.'

My answer was met with a cold stare. The subject of discussion changed.

'What do you want to do when you grow up?'

'I want to be a doctor,' I said proudly.

'Why is that?'

Shit, I've no idea. Silence; a long silence. Eventually, the headmaster volunteered,

'To help people?'

'Yes, I stammered, that's right, to help people.'

End of interview. I've blown it. I felt bad, really bad. I've let myself down and I've let my family down.

4

BEYOND SCHOOL

Piano lessons

Activities to keep me occupied outside school included piano lessons. Every Wednesday morning, I set off for school with my dedicated satchel containing my sheet music, leaving it in the porch at the house of my music teacher, Mrs Williams. After school, I returned for my lesson. I was a slow learner in spite of undertaking, religiously, my piano practise. I began to dread Wednesdays.

At one memorable lesson, my hands poised over the ivories (of which the keys were indeed carved), unsure of the next chord, I turned to look at Mrs Williams for guidance: she was in tears. My parents agreed I should not be inflicted on her any longer.

Just before I gave up the lessons, my family persuaded me to give a recital: I remember the piece to this day. I won praise from my sister, then aged just six:

'Quite good for his age, isn't he?'

Thank you, Sue.

I do miss the piano we owned, a player piano (often called a Pianola) with many rolls of music. A roll is inserted into the piano mechanism, the pedals pumped and the music plays. Look, no hands! With no space for the piano when we moved to Bristol many years later, the magnificent instrument was sold for a paltry £25.

I amuse myself nowadays playing simple pieces by ear. Reading sheet music was my downfall, caused in no small part by my poor eyesight.

Cub Scouts

At around 8-years-of-age, I was enrolled as a wolf cub, now more commonly known as cub scouts. After tea each Tuesday another one-mile walk – or more likely a run – back into town for pack night. I loved the relatively short time I was there. My financially-stretched parents were required to fork out for the uniform which included my necker (scarf) and woggle to hold the necker in place. Ah yes, the woggle, why did Baden Powell decide to call it that?

We were a full-sized pack, with six sixes and an amazing Akela who instructed us in all the usual skills, including tying knots, but the only knot I remember today is the reef knot. Learning a variety of skills was good, but we looked forward with great eagerness to those evenings when treated to a hunting trail around town.

A paper chase was frowned upon because of the litter it caused so the trail was marked out, by one of the sixers, with chalk marks on various buildings, telegraph poles and the like. An exciting – and healthy – time was enjoyed by us all.

Around November 5th we built a bonfire in the clearing in front of the scout hut, all of us mucking in. The fire was lit – a sign for a singsong! Some of the songs and mantras were, and still are, favourites. 'London's Burning' was sung regularly, but I particularly remember the 'Dinner Train' chant which replicated the sound of a train gathering speed along the track – before the days of continuous rail. The first verse is a slow repetition of coffee, coffee, coffee, coffee, followed by verses of increasing speed finalising with fish and chips, fish and chips, fish and chips, recited quickly.

Subs were voluntary. My parents gave me 6d (2½p) each week, but I noticed some boys contributed to the pack just 1d. I thought if I gave 3d, generous compared with some, I would have 3d left over for a bag of chips on the way home. I could use my money box to change the 6d into smaller denominations before setting out. So that's what I did.

Melksham Spa

Until my move to secondary school, our parents rented one of three large sprawling properties on Spa Road, Melksham. These houses were built in 1815 by the Melksham Spa Company as boarding houses for users of the newly discovered spa. The enterprise did not last long, no match for the strong competition from fashionable Bath, 13 miles distant.

Our house, 'Springfield', (an appropriate name), was a large grey austere building accessed by a circular gravel drive, spread over four levels and with a medley of outhouses, one of which became used as the kennel for a succession of dogs, including our beloved deerhound, Ailsa. The outhouses doubled up as excellent buildings for impromptu games of hide and seek and general mucking about.

I was fortunate our house lay on the outskirts of Melksham in a rural part of Wiltshire. We lived near a farm and during weekends and holidays, much time was spent there. We watched the dairy herd being milked (by hand), the milk then passing though the open-air milk cooler. We watched the farmer's wife making butter, all tasks undertaken with no hygiene regulations to be concerned about.

Many a happy hour we spent in the hay barn and the nearby tree-house the farmer built for his children. With others, I loved climbing up the ladder into the little house, that is until the day we found a large and very much alive snake in residence. We never went back.

Dad suffered an unfortunate experience at Springfield. Driving out on to the quiet main road at around 7.00 am one morning, late for work, possibly having been held up by one my mothers' rows with him, he didn't look out for passing traffic, knowing there wouldn't be any at that time of day. Well, there was that day. He knocked a motorcyclist off his machine, drawing blood. Dad rushed back to the house to call an ambulance, then ran back to the road to keep the injured rider company. He had disappeared. It was assumed his injuries were not as bad as they looked but, according to my father, they did look bad, very bad.

My first bicycle

At an early age I was given my first bicycle, not new of course, but new to me. I soon learnt to ride, cycling freely on all the country lanes and main roads, so quiet compared with today. I was, though, jealous of other boys – I envied their ability to ride 'no-hands' and I was really keen to learn the skill. I chose my opportunity to have a go at risking this challenge on a Sunday afternoon family bike outing.

I was riding in front of the rest of the family. After passing a parked car I stayed in the middle of the road, plenty of space either side of me and thought…Now's my chance! I took my hands off the handlebars. Within seconds, I was lying on the road with my family toppling on top of me. They were not best pleased. No head protection for any of us – it was to be many years before wearing cycle helmets became common.

Undaunted by this misfortune, a little later I attempted the trick again, this time alone. I soon mastered the task, proudly then able to demonstrate my new-found skills to both family and friends alike.

Later cycling adventures

One unforgettable day I suffered a most unpleasant experience. I was cycling innocently along our local leafy lane on a newer bike, on my way to explore the nearby river. The route took me past neighbours who owned a German Shepherd dog, Bruce. On this fateful day, Bruce took exception to me cycling past 'his' gate. He bit my leg. Badly. I knew I should tell my parents about this to receive whatever treatment may be necessary. I didn't. Why?

My brother Tony had recently been given a tetanus inoculation and suffered a very painful reaction. No way was I going to put myself up for a nasty injection and the likely accompanying pain. A scar developed on my leg. I maintained my silence even though the leg continued aching for several days after the event. An unfortunate incident – but I survived.

I was unlucky with the Bruce encounter as I cycled regularly for miles and miles around the area and into local towns, even Bath, suffering no mishaps with these excursions. I continued to explore Wiltshire, but never again would I cycle past the German Shepherd.

Later on, we moved to a cottage in Seend, a village just four miles from Melksham. More on this a little later. During my bike rides around the village I was intrigued to know how many households possessed a television set in the mid-1950s. Yes, I did create various hobbies and developed projects of much interest to me, of little concern to anyone else. On my travels, I counted how many houses were adorned with a TV aerial and how many not. I was unable to allow for buildings that might be split into flats, or indeed houses not visible from the road, but I came up with a result – about 50:50. Well, there you go.

In the mid-nineteenth century, Seend enjoyed a mini-industry. Iron ore was extracted from a site close to the village and sent to South Wales for smelting, first transported by barge using the Kennet and Avon Canal, then across the Bristol Channel. (The local pub beside the canal in Seend, now more a gastro pub, has always been called The Barge Inn). In later years the ore was transported by rail. The mine was short-lived but I mention this now because in the 1950s the mining site created a great place for mucking about on our bikes.

We kept clear of the canal, though. One frozen winter a boy, skating on thin ice, fell through and drowned. I believe there have been a couple of tragic drownings since.

Trips to Bristol

In the 1950s I possessed only one grandmother, a housekeeper to a clergyman in Bristol. Dad visited her regularly and, on a few occasions, I stayed with her for a few days to give me a change of scene, also I suspect, to give my parents a break. I so relished those visits. Each morning she cooked my favourite breakfast of chipolata sausages, the enticing aroma wafting up from the kitchen – an excellent way to get me out of bed.

I always spent a few days with her in early January, the prime reason for choosing this time of

41

year was to attend the annual church pantomime. I loved those shows, believing the humour to be brilliantly funny. My sights were set a little low. I joined in excitedly with every 'Oh yes he is' and 'He's behind you' and now take much pleasure in watching my younger grandchildren enjoying such shows; all great British humour.

My mother, though, could never be persuaded to watch any pantomime, thinking the whole idea silly and pointless. She wasn't blessed with a great sense of humour and indeed wasn't known for smiling much, unless she had a large glass of sherry in her hand.

For some of my time staying with my grandmother I was left on my own to catch up with my reading (comics yes, but also books) and to explore the local area, Sea Walls, Bristol Downs and the like. At least once during my visits we took a trip into Bristol city centre, catching the number 2 bus from Blackboy Hill. The same numbered bus still runs and on the same route today.

Gran had a fear of leaving the gas hob on when leaving the house. On one such trip to town, I thought it would be amusing to ask her, as we were about to board the bus, whether she had remembered to turn the gas off. She cursed (mildly, under her breath). There was no option but for us to trek back to the house and of course, she had turned off the gas. She was not amused.

Gran had shopping to do and we always took a walk through the Broadmead area of Bristol, admiring the construction of new buildings but also looking in wonder and dismay at the damage inflicted on the city throughout the Bristol Blitz of 1940/41. Those buildings not destroyed by Nazi bombs were being demolished to make way for development of the new shopping centre.

Just a short walk from Gran's house was a cave, high up in the Avon Gorge, called by us 'The Grotto'. On a weekend summer's day, the whole family might make a day trip to Bristol to enjoy a picnic in the grotto, admiring the breath-taking views. Allegedly, J M W Turner visited the spot to paint the views both up and down the gorge.

Gran's house is long gone but 'our grotto' is very much still there, now privately owned, but recently I returned for a clandestine visit and reminded myself of those splendid family picnics – and the magnificent views.

Long trousers – or not

Short trousers – the norm until secondary school. I was though, after much pleading, promised a pair of long trousers for my 11th birthday party as I would be moving to my secondary education a few months later. At school, I told my friends to expect me to

43

be so attired but the trousers never materialised. My pals arrived at the party exclaiming in unison:

'Chris, where are the long trousers!'

A bit embarrassing but fortunately all the other boys were also still wearing shorts. I cannot remember the reason my parents gave for not fulfilling their promise, but I suspect it had something to do with money – or rather the lack of it.

Now older, I look forward to summer holidays, giving me the opportunity to willingly, and happily, wear shorts. Not a pretty sight, some might say.

5

A MOVE OF HOUSE

At around the time I left primary school, we moved house, from Melksham to a tumbledown cottage in nearby Seend, briefly mentioned earlier. My parents were grateful – and lucky – to be granted a mortgage despite the dilapidated state of the property. The cottage was named by my parents as 'Little Acre'. The grounds amounted to less than half an acre but still a good-sized plot.

Major improvements were necessary, not least the provision of a bathroom and an inside toilet to replace the privy halfway down the garden. In earlier days, for reasons of health and general well-being, it was common for lavatories to be situated outside the property.

'What, 'ave the facilities and all them germs indoors, dear? No way, we can't be 'avin that!'

The privy was a twin-seater. I can only imagine it was the custom in 'olden days' for husband and wife to share the morning ritual, no doubt to discuss the forthcoming tasks of the day. No mains drainage for the privy, just a soakaway. As this facility became something of a talking point, we kept it, even after the installation of indoor conveniences. On the quiet, I used it occasionally, just for a pee, mind, not solids…

A builder was employed for structural alterations. In confident manner Mr. Daly reassured us:
    'Six weeks max. my friend, no sweat.'
    Six *months* later we started to see the end of this phase of development drawing into sight and it would now be down to my father to take over. He would be exerting a lot of sweat.

Dad managed a tobacco factory in Devizes. He habitually dressed in a three-piece suit and stiff collar, five-and-a-half long days each week, with just two weeks annual leave. Notwithstanding this onerous commitment to his job, he decorated the entire cottage, with some help from Mum, built a garage, a workshop, and landscaped the spacious gardens.

I am told that when I saw him working on all this, I had the irritating habit of asking him what he was *trying* to do, rather than asking what he was actually doing. Absolutely no malice on my part, it was just my way of making polite conversation.

During renovations, the tiny Victorian hearth in the main living room was removed to reveal, to my parents' surprise, a glorious inglenook fireplace. The open fire was fuelled with logs from trees cleared from the rambling gardens, topped up with smoky coal. One downside to this homely scene, apart from smoke sometimes billowing into the living room, was that the chimney needed regular sweeping. Never one to shirk a challenge, Dad purchased a set of chimney brushes to do the job himself, several times, until the day we moved out of the cottage several years later.

All this labouring on the cottage was not without some cost to Dad's health. Due to his low blood pressure he fainted several times, thankfully not when driving. On many a night he returned home late, exhausted and physically drained. Nevertheless, however tired he felt, he always found time to work on various chores around the property.

As an example of his commitment to his job, each Christmas he wrote a personal letter of thanks to every one of his over 100 employees at the factory. The stress of his job often led to illness, but with his conscientious nature he resolutely forced himself back to work, often only to fall seriously ill later, necessitating home visits from our family doctor and, more than once, extended time off work. The cumulative result of all this eventually led to his early retirement on health grounds. He continued to suffer ill health until the day he died, but, considering his history, lived to the very reasonable ripe old age of 86 years.

As the building work and improvements cost far more than originally budgeted, funds did not run to any form of central heating. So it was that on cold winter mornings ice formed on the inside of the single-glazed bedroom windows, an experience shared with many hardy souls who lived at the time. Heating the cottage, apart from the main living room which benefited from the open fireplace, was considered an unnecessary luxury.

My bedroom

I was fortunate in being allocated my own bedroom and allowed to personalise the room. This included displaying on the walls, maps of the continents of the world, these holding a particular fascination for me.

I built a gravity-fed miniature railway using the rails from our electric train set together with my collection of marbles. It was quite impressive, even if I say so myself.

When in bed, I was inquisitive to hear what was going on in the cottage (likely to be arguments outside my bedroom or elsewhere). So I assembled a contraption of string and pulleys to open and close the bedroom door from the comfort of my bed, located on the opposite side of the room. A fiddle to operate, it would certainly have been much easier to hop out of bed to operate the door, but not so much fun. The arrangement kept me amused for a while.

I was feeling particularly happy (for a change), very contented with my own bedroom, my belongings around me and excited, if in trepidation, about a new school adventure beckoning. One day I casually remarked to my parents:

'It's alright here, I like it, I don't think I'll leave home when I grow up.'

I imagine they murmured in reply,

'We'll see about that.'

6

SECONDARY SCHOOL

In spite of the Eleven-Plus interview cock-up I was offered a place at the grammar school, Trowbridge Boys High School (TBHS), the same seat of learning my brother Tony was already attending. In September 1956 I moved to 'Big School': onwards and upwards.

A typical school day started with preparing my breakfast, usually cereal in the summer, porridge in the winter. The porridge was left on the stove overnight, creating a fairly solid mixture. I ladled a dollop into a bowl, added milk and if I gently rotated the bowl, the porridge floated on the milk. I still do this…It doesn't take a lot to entertain me. I am aware not everyone adds milk to their bowl of porridge – they are missing all the fun.

Breakfast was followed first by a brisk walk to the bottom of the garden, in summer picking an apple, pear or strawberry or two, depending on what was in the well-stocked fruit garden. Then over the stile, across the field to the main road and the bus stop for the 7.55 am service to Trowbridge. I was one of the first to arrive at school, at around 8.20 am, the bus running only hourly.

Tony, maybe because he was in his teens, always rose late. He habitually missed breakfast, running across the field at speed to catch the new Routemaster bus. He became well known to the conductors on the route and the bus waited for him if the conductor spotted him running across the field. If not seen, he missed the bus. This happened on many occasions. Bus conductors are now virtually extinct so in similar circumstances today, Tony would invariably miss the bus and be late for school, exposing himself to reprimand, or quite possibly something worse.

My first day

I was kitted out in the compulsory school uniform, including the school badge stitched to the front pocket of the blazer, together with the regulation navy blue school cap. Caps were worn only by first years' and for the more daring boys, only for the first term. Headgear was not considered 'cool', or whatever was the expression of the time.

I liked my first day at my new school, intrigued with the gentle indoctrination into their procedures, rules and regulations. The bell at the end of each lesson was new to me.

On this first day, our form master told us of one new boy who suffered from haemophilia, not that that was the word used. He explained that the boy in question if cut could bleed uncontrollably. If a fight appeared imminent we were to walk away quietly. To identify the boy without causing him unnecessary embarrassment, he was to be given a message to bring to our form master. Very soon, a boy entered the room, handed the master a piece of paper and left.

'That wasn't him!', we were told.

A few minutes later another boy entered with another note.

'That's him,' mouthed the master.

The boy was small, pasty-faced with blond hair. I forget his name.

An aside on my friend Philip

Philip moved with me from primary school to Trowbridge High. He was high spirited, not a term his mother used.

'There's high spirits in some boys, Philip, but that's not you. You are just downright disobedient.'

I can give one example of Philip's behaviour. At the bottom of their large overgrown garden, a high stone wall ran along the rear of various neighbours' gardens. A hobby of Phil's was to climb the wall, crawl along and make rude gestures at the neighbours. One elderly nearby resident was having none of this and cemented milk bottles along the top of his section of the wall. Philip duly smashed the lot and continued, unabated, to harass his long-suffering neighbours. He was often called 'a very naughty boy.'

He was undeniably a tearaway with no fear of punishment, running his long-suffering mother ragged. When it all became too much for her, she hid away with a cup of tea and her copy of the *Daily Chronicle* (trivia alert – the paper disappeared at the end of the 1950s, absorbed into the *Daily Mail*.)

Now and again I spent an overnight at Philip's house (not called a sleepover then, just 'I stayed the night'). I liked his mum: she was very pleasant and kind-hearted towards me. Maybe I appeared polite and well-manned compared to her wayward son.

I was introduced to new experiences – one teatime she introduced me to junket. Being forever hungry I was always happy to try any new food. I loved it, a pudding that was never served at home. It might be interesting to try it again but like many dishes today, I would very certainly find it too sweet for my taste.

Breakfast at their house consisted of cereal and toast. Full fat milk was the regular order. I learnt that each day the family took turns to enjoy 'Tom' – top-of-milk, the rich milk at the top of the bottle. Fresh toast was provided but Philip's dad insisted we wait for the toast to cool before spreading the butter. An economical family, as all families were. To spread the butter on hot toast – well, you tended to just use more.

What I found surprising about Philip was that he could, when in the right mood, behave well at school, although he was never to be a model pupil. Yes, two sides to him, but it was the misbehaving side usually in evidence.

Beyond the first school day

We were introduced to proper timetables. All the usual subjects – English, Mathematics, History, Geography, Sciences and, perhaps surprising for a grammar school with the emphasis on academia – Woodwork. I was probably about average on the traditional subjects but clearly didn't excel at the woodworking class. Eventually, the master-in-charge suggested, quite gently, he didn't think I possessed a natural aptitude in the subject. I readily agreed.

I was happy with the timetable, not that there was any choice in the early years of secondary education, but Wednesday afternoons were something else – the dreaded (for me) so-called 'Games' afternoon. I was happy with summer athletics, reasonably good at sprinting (100 yards) and hurdling which I enjoyed, yet I possessed absolutely no interest nor talent in field team sports. It helps to be able to see the ball, my poor eyesight being rather a hindrance as, understandably, I was not allowed to wear my glasses on the field.

As I said, the school was a grammar school but the headmaster upheld ideas above his station, trying to model the establishment along the lines of a public school.

We were split into four houses with competitions between us, playing rugby in the winter term, football in the spring, cricket in the summer. I hated all of it.

I was not against exercise in principle, in fact I rather liked the easy walk from Trowbridge bus station to the school in Wingfield Road, a distance of just under a mile. Not surprisingly, the walk after school was more enjoyable than the morning walk when burdened with the thought of a whole school day ahead. To add variety and speed to the journey without adding too much exertion, I was introduced to the concept of running for twenty paces, then walk for twenty, and so on. In my dotage I have been known to repeat this on my morning walks. But not that often.

A new concept for me at 'Big School' was the tuck shop – sweets, chocolate and crisps readily available during every break, a popular venue for us all. In season, apples featured but fruit did not hold the same attraction as Mars Bars and the like.

The school staff

The school masters were a mixed bunch. 'Gus' Bucknell, the head, an enthusiastic admirer of Shakespeare and caner-in-chief. His nickname evolved from his name – GVS Bucknell. Gus, alone among the teaching staff, regularly wore his gown but not his mortar board.

Other masters included 'Fizz' Kemery, a weak individual who to our shame we teased cruelly, and Mr Powell, an evil little man who sought every opportunity to mete out punishment. Unfortunately for him, only the head could use the cane – but Powell made up for this disappointment in other ways, painful ways.

Most masters – although not all – were decent men. One agreeable and popular master, I forget his name, possessed a good-natured sense of humour.

On entering the unruly form room one morning, some wag piped up:

'Backs to the wall, lads!'

'Ok, boys, return to your desks now, please,' he said with a patient smile.

On this subject, I was unaware of any sexual malpractices by the school masters. Not to say they weren't any, mind.

The masters were always addressed as 'Sir'. They all had nicknames but none of us was brave or foolish enough to use them to their face.

For ourselves, we used various terms of endearment such as four-eyes for the bespectacled, girl or girlie occasionally, homo was a regular favourite. Sometimes name-calling became stronger using four-letter words, but all names were used in good spirit. Well, usually.

Watch your spelling

As the school was a grammar school, we were expected to take our education seriously, with predominant attention being given to the English language, particularly spelling. Our English master, 'Stew' Prosser, once intercepted a note passed between two boys. Michael, good-heartedly and without any malice, tried to pass a jokey note to another boy, which read:

'You're a lesbin.'

Mr Prosser held up the note, querying:

'What's a 'lesbin?',

thereby, unfortunately for Michael, drawing attention to his poor spelling. He was put in the sin bin for that, not for the content of the note but for the poor spelling. He remained sitting in the corner of the classroom with legs crossed and hands-on-head for the regulatory ten minutes.

Am Dram

Then there was drama class, which included performing in front of the form. In one particular production I played the part of a middle-aged woman, with another boy playing a male role. We read and acted through the script which was fine until a page was turned and we were faced with an instruction at the top of the next page – *they embrace*. Horror of horrors, were we expected to kiss? We fumbled an awkward clinch. One of the more embarrassing and well-remembered incidents at school.

Uncomfortable as that was, it did not stop me, even perchance encouraged me later in life (the 1970s) to immerse myself – willingly – in amateur dramatics. One of many characters I played was

Friar Tuck in our Christmas pantomime. In another role, the script instructed that I run across the stage with my trousers falling to my ankles (Sir Percy Shorter in *Habeas Corpus*). All good fun. In truth, rehearsals were more enjoyable than the actual performances as, on the night, it was only right and proper to do our best to give value for money to our long-suffering paying audience.

School toilets – a must to avoid

During this period of my development I was quite introverted, although not too shy to raise my hand if, during lessons, I needed a loo visit. I did this only once as I invariably took care to relieve myself at break time. Not like a most unfortunate fellow pupil, sadly no longer with us, desperate for a pee but too embarrassed to raise his hand. He flooded the classroom floor.

The toilets were disgusting (until the building of a new block in 1958) and known as 'the bogs'. I thought this expression unique to our school and it was to be a while before I became educated otherwise and learnt this was (and is) very much a universal term. We never spent longer than absolutely necessary in the old toilets, goodness knows what diseases and illnesses we could have succumbed to in that hellhole. Further, a boy must be desperate to sit on the seat – or more likely on the grubby, suspiciously stained pan, as most toilet seats were missing.

Once the new block was built, we enjoyed altogether much cleaner, less smelly facilities. It was then not unknown for certain boys to loiter therein and, huddled together furtively with fertile imagination, share information about what filled the minds of 13- and 14-year-old boys.

On the question of diseases, at secondary school the authorities lost interest in checking for head lice and flat feet, but instead inoculations became all the rage, particularly for polio and TB, both painful. Blood tests were taken for TB: a negative result for me.

Sex education

I found many lessons at school to be boring, habitually finding difficulty in maintaining my concentration but, naturally enough for a young boy, I suffered no such difficulty in focusing on our sex education lessons.

These lasted the entire morning of one memorable day. We were 13- and 14-year-olds (late on today's standards to being versed in the subject). Doctor Matthews put us at our ease by including a joke during his lecture. He explained that while giving his question and answer session on a recent school visit, he was asked how often a couple might have sex:

'When young, this might be three or four times a week but when old, perhaps only once a year.'

On hearing this, the elderly school matron sitting in the corner of the room was heard to say excitedly, in a stage whisper:

'Yes, next Tuesday!'

The good doctor didn't include what was later to become my favourite joke on the subject…Two elderly residents in a care home were planning to get married. The gentleman asked his fiancée what she thought about sex.

'I would like it infrequently,' she replied. After a pause, he enquired:

'Is that one word or two?'

At morning break, we were invited to place anonymous questions in a box provided by Doctor Matthews, who promised to give his answers on our return to the room. There were some *very* explicit questions placed in the box that day.

He limited his talk to mainstream sexual issues with no mention of other traits. It was to be decades before LGBT would be openly discussed at school or elsewhere. Today, all aspects of the subject are taught, even to young primary school pupils. A step too far, considered by some.

Never a word on the subject did I receive from my parents.

Time for a smoke

Smoking was very much a way of life in the 1950s with a large majority of men – and women – participating. We were keen to take part in the habit. So at an early age we started experimenting, an exciting pursuit strictly banned at school. Initially, this was just a summer term activity. On fine days during the lunch break a group of us would collect dried grass from the playing field to make roll-ups, using a Rizla rolling machine and packets of cigarette papers bought in town. We smoked the result: quite disgusting. If the sun was shining, we set light to any remaining dried grass using our schoolboy magnifying glasses. Happy days indeed.

We later graduated to the real thing, *Woodbines* and *Dominos* usually our cigarette of choice, not in any way considered pleasant, but they were cheap.

It was no surprise that before long our playing field fledgling tobacco enterprise was noticed. We received a summons to report to the headmaster at morning break the following day. Some of our fellow pupils, not involved in our misdemeanours, thought it amusing to barricade us in our classroom at the set time, thereby causing us to miss the appointment. The worry this caused me might have led to it being *my* turn to pee my pants.

As soon as we managed to escape, we ran to attend the now sorely delayed meeting with the head, making our apologies that we had 'forgotten'. He waved us away without a word and more surprisingly, no punishment. Was he aware of the reason for our delay, I wonder?

School sports

The autumn term heralded the feared exposure to 'Games' on Wednesday afternoons I touched on earlier. I have always been happy watching rugby and football, live or on television, but having to play such sports was always the low point of the week for me.

An exception to my hatred of sporting activities was gymnastics and I enjoyed joining my house for circuit training in the gym. The best bit for me became the pommel horse (without bars) which I did enjoy, being half-decent at it.

One day, Graham, a precocious boy with Lord Fauntleroy hair, misjudged his run at the horse and landed on his bum, grinning at the rest of us. After a short pause, our PT instructor asked:

'Graham, are you an only child?'

He was in truth just that, the instructor deducing this fact from Graham's spoilt-child demeanour.

Boxing was also on the curriculum. The instructor nominated me as timekeeper for this so-called sport, as with my poor eyesight I would be at no small disadvantage boxing without my glasses. I was glad of the excuse.

Sickness – and snow

I suppose all these compulsory sporting pursuits were intended to develop us into healthy and hearty young men but I am not sure if any of the activities made a great difference to our state of health or mind. The school suffered a substantial amount of sickness while I was there. I endured a perpetual cold and infections throughout much of my school education, the earlier removal of my tonsils having made little or no difference.

There was no escape from the Asian flu epidemic in the 1950s. I was one of many struck down and, an event surprising today, I received a house call from our family doctor. On my return to school after a week in bed, I learnt that over 100 boys were absent at any one time, a third of the school. That was a nasty bug.

The plus side to the depths of winter was snow, sometimes quite a lot of it. Opposite our cottage was a sloping field, ideal for tobogganing. On any day when snow settled (or 'pitched' in Wiltshire speak), I jumped off the homeward-bound school bus, ran to the shed, collected my sledge and rushed to the field. Darkness might be falling but the snow reflected what light there was to illuminate trees and other nasty obstacles. There I remained, happy with my own company until called in for tea.

Accidents will happen

Perhaps every school has one particularly accident-prone pupil. We had Peter Cornish. On the day the booby-trapped blackboard and easel fell to the floor, rather than trapping a schoolmaster it was going to be Peter standing underneath. He suffered a very nasty blow to his head, leading to time off school.

That incident was later surpassed by a summer athletics day on the school playing field, one activity being the shot put, known to us as 'putting the shot'. Why did Peter have to wander into range to be knocked unconscious by a shot hitting the side of his head? This was serious for Peter, dramatic for the rest of us as we watched an ambulance racing across the field. Peter was lifted on a stretcher and taken to A & E. Bad news for him and the incident was no doubt a bit upsetting for the poor boy who threw that particular shot.

Peter lost a large chunk of his schooling that year. He did in time make a full recovery from the injury, although he suffered poor health throughout his school days, regularly missing school for weeks at a time.

A safer activity on the playing field during break time was the popularity of throwing Frisbees, at least this was a popular activity until the flying discs were confiscated 'on safety grounds'. But no-one at school was ever injured by a Frisbee, unlike the shot…

Our school desks – these comprised a desk and seat joined as one unit by metal runners, purpose-built for playing 'shunting trains' when no teaching staff were around; a popular activity until an unfortunate accident. During one rather vigorous game, the runners of one desk unit snapped, the two sections falling apart, landing upended on the floor. Disaster! What have we done? The four of us held a committee meeting and decided we best own up or there would be hell to pay for our classmates. And honesty pays, doesn't it?

We spoke to the school secretary to ask to see the headmaster. After waiting with increasing fear, eventually she showed us into his study where we confessed our crime.

'What on earth were you playing at? I shall have to think about this. Come back tomorrow at the same time.'

The next day we returned, in trepidation.

'Well, boys, it's going to cost a pound to repair, that's five bob from each of you.'

No beatings, just the cost of the repair, five shillings (25p) each for playing trains that day. As we had done the honourable thing in owning up to our misbehaviour, we thought that a bit harsh. Five shillings! – big money for us. Still, we might have received six of the best, or at least detention so, all-in-all, we should have been grateful. I expect we were.

Acknowledging my various misconducts and lack of commitment to study, I received only a few detentions and one of those was not my fault, honest, but general misbehaving, remaining in school buildings during break-time, skiving off games and the rest, undoubtedly were my fault and those detentions I did deserve.

Crime and punishment

Let the punishment fit the crime (W. S. Gilbert)

I was not so lucky at the end of one summer term, after a particularly bad school report. My underachievement led to my first – thankfully only – caning from the head. I was warned on an earlier occasion that if I didn't knuckle down and concentrate on my education, I would be facing corporal punishment. Naturally I ignored this sound advice. I was conscientious about handing home-work in on time but this was always rushed, resulting in generally poor results.

It is a truth universally acknowledged that a young boy in possession of a reluctance to study must be in need of a punishment. Canings for poor work were carried out on one of the last days of term. The appointed day arrived. I was in no doubt what was coming my way and what was to be my fate. In readiness, I emptied my bladder several times that morning. Shortly before lunch break the head's secretary popped her head round the classroom door, looked directly at me, and said:

'The headmaster will see you now.'

I rose from my desk and walked to the door with 29 pairs of eyes watching me. They knew. The form master, buried in his notes, also knew. I arrived at the head's study and knocked timidly on the door.

'Enter!'

No further words were spoken as he opened a cupboard to reveal a wide assortment of canes. Why so many? He rummaged through the collection and selected one. Christ, I thought, that looks lethal. He pointed to a chair and, still silent, indicated that he expected me to 'bend over', placing his hand on my back. The punishment was carried out. He released me and immediately I shot to the door to make my escape. As I was leaving, I ran into the secretary who was entering the room, causing her to spill the cup of coffee she was bringing the headmaster. She gave me a black look, muttering:

'Oh dear, I shall have to make another one now.'

I started to make my way back to lessons, but first a detour to the loo and a feel of my sore bum. I collected my thoughts, took a deep breath and returned to the form room to face the enquiring looks on the faces of my classmates.

My parents never knew of the punishment and would have been shocked as – in their view – I was not a troublemaker, although they might have guessed that in reading my poor school report for that term, I deserved a little ticking off.

Our school masters were respected, partly because it was right to do so but, more particularly, because we all lived under constant fear of corporal punishment. No such punishment today, yet it is argued by some that without that deterrent comes a lack of respect for teaching staff. Perhaps there should be a campaign to bring back the cane. Or perhaps not.

Other punishments were carried out daily, a slap or two with a ruler across the palm of the hand being popular with several masters. Humiliating for some, bravado for others. No way could we tell our mums and dads when being so admonished, for fear of parental repercussions. Detentions were different – parents would have to be given the reason for being kept late in school, unless the transgressor was able to invent a water-tight, feasible story to explain the late homecoming.

I escaped the ruler, but on numerous occasions was set 'lines' for misbehaving in the classroom, such as talking out of turn, trying to get a rise out of the form master and similar wrong-doings. I felt lines to be a fairly pointless exercise. Surely, time spent on this penance could be more profitably employed in school community service, such as sweeping the playground and the like. The converse to this is that being set hundreds of lines did improve my handwriting. Today, unfortunately, this has reverted to a scrawl.

So, plenty of punishments were handed out but the school suffered little in the way of bullying. On occasions, smaller boys might be tormented with the threat of having their head pushed down the lavatory bowl, followed by the chain being pulled to flush the loo. (In explanation for the younger reader, a chain was used then, not a handle). This practise did happen but albeit rarely, as far as I knew; shades of *Tom Brown's Schooldays*. I was never the giver nor, thankfully, the receiver of such treatment.

Nowadays, a high-level flush operated by a chain can be a much sought-after feature for the modern bathroom, particularly in an older period property. What goes around comes around?

We learnt to keep quiet at school on our birthday. Should the fact be discovered, we ran the risk of exposing ourselves to receiving 'The Bumps'. This was painful and if carried out vigorously might be dangerous, but was not classified as bullying.

I was not bullied at school, but when on holiday I suffered at the hands of bullies a couple of times, more of which later.

Academically, my achievements during autumn and spring terms were considered at best average, but invariably I turned in a mediocre or even bad performance during summer terms. Outdoor attractions were far more rewarding than dull and uninteresting school lessons and homework.

On at least two occasions, I was placed 'On Report', nominally for the first two weeks of the autumn term but in reality, as long as it took for my behaviour and academic performance to improve. This procedure entailed the issue each Monday morning of a report sheet which listed every lesson period for each day of the week. At the end of each lesson, I was required to ask the form tutor to 'sign me off'.

One natural history lesson covered aquatic plants, and towards the end of the session our tutor showed us an example of elodea. I called out with a smile, 'Hello dear!' This won me a rare round of laughter from my fellow pupils but also a bad mark on my report sheet that day.

The fairer sex

Apart from cleaning and catering staff, just two ladies worked at the school, the headmaster's secretary and the school nurse. I guess female teaching staff at a school for boys was not considered appropriate or fitting in those distant days.

A story about the school nurse, a fearsome woman: one day she addresses a group of schoolboys:

'Has anyone seen Mike Hunt?'

This elicited various rude replies:

'Not recently, Miss,' or

'Are you offering, Miss?'

It is mildly amusing to think this happened at my school, but unlikely, although a boy with such a name was indeed there. It is, of course, a play on words that's been around for a while and was used in the 1981 teen comedy film 'Porky's'.

As I mentioned in my first book, I was a late developer with my interaction with members of the fairer sex, in likelihood caused in part by attending a boys-only school for my secondary education. (The school, now co-educational – probably a good thing – has amalgamated with other schools in the vicinity to create a large comprehensive).

At around 13-years-of-age I started to think, even dream, that maybe girls might not be such a bad thing after all and, in the company of others, I waved to girls at their school on the opposite side of the hedge separating the two gender-divided schools. We were not allowed too close to the hedge, the intention being to protect the girls from any unwanted attention. That was probably quite unnecessary, acknowledging our immaturity.

I waved occasionally to a girl I knew, Heather, her parents being close friends of mine. With slowly growing confidence, a little later I cautiously approached another girl, Ann, a shy and diminutive fair maiden (I assumed) with amazingly beautiful long blonde hair. On a couple of occasions we met after school and walked together, but not hand-in-hand, to the bus station, chatting intermittently and awkwardly. Well, you have to start somewhere.

A digression – these memories remind me of a rare girl encounter at home, the evening my parents invited our family doctor, Dr Bruce-Kyloe, and his wife Daphne to dinner, well after my bedtime. First,

I need to give an explanatory note on family bedtimes. Our parents were firm believers in the old proverb, allegedly first quoted by Benjamin Franklin:

> *Early to bed, early to rise,*
> *Makes a man healthy, wealthy and wise.*

On this basis, bedtimes were set at 7.00 pm for my younger sister, 8.00 pm for myself and 9.00 pm for my older brother, but we were allowed to read in bed for a while. These timings were not strictly enforced and later on, bedtimes drifted, but on the night of the Bruce-Kyloe's visit I was in bed soon after 8.00 pm.

I was initially unaware that the doctor and his good lady had brought along their young daughter, Fiona, knowing we were the same age and would remember each other, having been in the same class at primary school. Whatever was the time for *her* bedtime? She came up to my bedroom and at the door was startled to find me in bed. I waved, smiling weakly at her, whereupon she returned to the dinner party. Embarrassment all round.

A personable, attractive girl and had we been a year older I would not have been in bed and conceivably we might have enjoyed a fumbled kiss or a cuddle. (Probably just wishful thinking). But nothing was going to happen that night, thanks to

74

my lack of experience with girls and her parents being entertained downstairs.

Swimming lessons

I am grateful to the school for teaching me to swim. We were marched to the local pool once a week and after a few lessons, I accomplished the required 10-yard swim, albeit achieved in a semi-circle rather than a straight line. Still, I was awarded my Learners Certificate, my first ever certificate which I still have to this day.

A swimming Gala was held each summer, a competition between the four houses in the school. One summer Gala is particularly memorable.

I was not up to standard to represent our house, so instead was seated with other non-competing boys – and parents – on one side of the pool. Before the start of the competition, the contestants lined up on the opposite side of the pool, wearing what today are known as 'speedos', for photographs. One boy who shall remain nameless, because I cannot recollect his name, for some reason became somewhat aroused. Much giggling, exchanged glances between us and embarrassed glances between parents. He was suspended from the competition and given detention the following day for his, no doubt, involuntary display. Bit harsh?

The pool incidentally, is long gone, now a supermarket.

After school

During summer terms I was allowed to cycle to school, some seven miles distant. I regularly met up with another Chris who lived at Hilperton on the outskirts of Trowbridge. I wait on my bike outside his house, he waves from the front window and moments later joins me to continue our journey to school together.

At school, we believed Chris to be 'grown-up for his age', being a font of knowledge, particularly matters of interest to young boys, and he regularly informed us of stimulating facts not included in the authorised school curriculum. At the time, we believed all of it.

For some reason we did not share the journey home at the end of the school day. He appeared reluctant to join me. I never knew why but conceivably because I was always looking for distractions after school whereas Chris might have been keen to get home for his tea. Or work on his homework – never a priority for me.

On fine days after school with no bus to catch, I took my time cycling home, regularly visiting the swimming pool with a friend or two. After the swim, when funds allowed, we bought a glass of warm, sweetened orange squash and a packet of the latest savoury invention, cheese and onion crisps. We considered these to be a vast improvement on the only choice until then, the flavourless *Smiths Crisps*, each bag containing that little blue wrap of salt (if lucky, two).

It is obvious homework did not weigh heavily on me during summer terms and this attitude played a significant part in my regular poor performance at school. This was the time of year for a variety of pastimes and activities, many in the fresh country air.

A favourite after-school pursuit was to spend time in the large rambling garden at the house of a close school friend, David. In the autumn, we collected conkers for contests at school, nothing unusual about that. Some boys claimed to boil their conkers in vinegar to make them longer lasting; I'm not sure that made any difference.

We climbed trees, rode our bikes and such like, but best of all was playing with fire. A large pile of broken sheets of asbestos was stored in the garden at David's house (yes, asbestos, this being long before the risk of asbestosis was full understood). We built a barbecue with this material, but even more fun was building what we called our rocket launching site. David, more technically gifted than me, could create a 'rocket' using cardboard or plastic tubing, filled with a combustible mixture including sodium chlorate. We then lit the homemade touch-paper, stood back and launched our rocket into space, or at least to the height of the surrounding trees. On occasions, a hapless spider or such-like might be given their trip of a lifetime.

David owned an airgun and a never-ending supply of pellets. It is with regret I admit the garden bird population might have become marginally reduced, thanks to our behaviour. But not a lot, we were poor shots. This activity was not noticed by David's parents but a couple of broken windows most certainly were.

Some evenings and weekends, friends came to me. We built ourselves a little house using a large stack of old bricks and discarded doors from the cottage renovations: this became our private den. A great place for illicit smoking, all good fun in fine weather, not so good after rain when the den flooded.

Close to our cottage was a steep hill leading down to a farm and working watermill. David came up with the bright idea for us, in turn, to ride down the hill on my sisters' tricycle, as a change from riding our bikes. David rode first, building up such speed he became unable to control the trike, hitting the wall of the farmhouse, full-on. The scene is still vivid in my mind. He did survive the escapade but my sister was not best pleased to have her tricycle written off in such a fashion. I was also a bit miffed as I didn't get to have a go on the trike that day.

Summer afternoons at the end of school were a delight, a welcome release from the challenges and boredom we faced throughout the day. I reflect on those enchanted times with warmth in my heart and perhaps the hint of a tear in my eye. In my memory the sun was always shining. But there was one afternoon, a horrific day with much sorrow which will live with me forever.

Paul Webb, not in my form although I knew of him, cycling home one day after school pulled out of a side road on to Stallard Street in Trowbridge, a busy main road. He was hit and run over by a petrol tanker. I was there moments after the tragedy and was traumatised, being faced with the scene of body parts littering the road. For a few seconds I believed this to be produce fallen from a butcher's delivery van until the full horror of the situation hit me. A school memorial service was held the following morning for Paul. Rarely were we subdued but we were that day.

7

FAMILY LIFE

The Good Old Days

Not always so good, particularly during the long, cold winters. We lived with fog, pea-soupers and smog, exacerbated by coal fires. Eventually various Clean Air Acts were passed, particularly the act ratified in 1968 which led to the popularity of anthracite, a smokeless high-density coal. A walk outdoors in a 1950s winter, particularly in the more built-up areas, could be grim – and very unhealthy, especially for the lungs.

In some ways, though, the late 1940s and the 1950s were relatively happy times for us living in Wiltshire. And expectations remained low.

Some years ago, I came across a poem written by a gentleman known as 'Pensioner Fenton' and I think this gives a flavour of the times. I read the poem at my parents' golden wedding party:

We met and we married a long time ago
We worked for long hours when wages were low
No holidays abroad, no carpets on floors
We didn't have money, did all our own chores

Our children arrived in those difficult days
And we brought them all up with little state aid
They were safe going out to play in the park
And old folk were safe going out in the dark

No vandals, no muggings, there was nothing to rob
We felt well off with a couple of bob
No Valium, no drugs, no LSD
We cured all our ills with a good cup of tea

And as we look back since the time we were wed
We think of the problems and the tears that were shed
But people were happy in those olden days
Always kind and caring in so many ways

'Awe, shucks, it did us good, life were grand, eh love?'

Not all might agree.

The poem maybe paints an overly cheerful picture of life in the years after the war, but it was received well by Mum and Dad. A favourite saying during the 1950s:

'What we don't have we don't miss.'

Not strictly true, of course, we did indeed miss those many luxuries that were well outside our household budget.

Housework

It was unusual for a housewife with children to have a job outside the home, certainly not a full-time job, having plenty to keep her busy. Housework was heavy going for the 1950s housewife. No washing machine nor tumble drier in our case, let alone a dishwasher.

Before the move to Seend when we invested in a twin-tub washing machine, clothes were washed in a large sink in the scullery, then wrung out by hand and fed through a green-painted mangle. Finally, in fine weather the washed garments were placed on the outside clothes line. On wet days, the horizontal clothes horse in the scullery would be brought into use, first loaded then hauled to the ceiling using a contraption of rope pulleys. Hard work.

Later, we became the proud owners of a vacuum cleaner, an incredibly efficient heavy-duty genuine Hoover, nothing like the modern plastic equivalent. No more hanging carpets in the back yard to be given an energetic hammering with the carpet beater. Fitted carpets were unknown in the Fifties.

We discovered *Dabitoff*, a cleaning fluid sold in a small bottle with a sponge in the neck. This was in almost daily use for removing stains on a variety of garments. I suspect the contents – then – were little more than basic white spirit, but it was effective. The product is still available today in a variety of containers, but not in the distinctive green and yellow bottle I remember.

Housework was very labour intensive and my mother hired 'a woman who does' who called twice a week to help out. She happily 'did for us' and was employed despite money being tight. No doubt old Mrs Alford was paid little for her hard graft.

She stopped for her 'elevenses', an expression I knew about; my mother invariably joined her for a cup of tea, a biscuit and a chat. This break from household chores usually took place soon after 10.00 am. If in the house at the time I was in the habit of exclaiming:

'Mummy, it's not 11 o'clock yet!'

I receive a 'be quiet' look.

Catering for the family

Cooking was a major time-consuming activity, so different to today. Economy was the abiding rule.

83

Mum's home-made ice cream was delicious, but I was not so keen on her economical combination of margarine and butter mixed 50:50 in her Kenwood.

Very little processed or convenience food was in evidence, with meals prepared from scratch. For those families lucky enough to have a garden, vegetables and fruit were grown, supplemented with whatever was available from local shops. In town, there was always a well-stocked greengrocer, a butcher, a baker and a general store, all providing basic ingredients for healthy eating. With no fridge at the Melksham house, food was stored in the pantry (a small room), later at the cottage at Seend in a larder cupboard.

That mention of home-grown fruit – the availability of several cooking-apple trees in our garden, coupled with careful storage of the produce, ensured a ready supply of the apples for much of the year. This led to 'stewed apples and custard' being our pudding of no choice most days. Due to this constant repetition, I grew to thoroughly dislike the dish – and still do. Apple sauce, though, very similar to stewed apple, is delicious with a generous portion of succulent roast pork, with or without the trimmings.

Garbage, including food scraps, was all deposited in the dustbin, domestic wheelie-bins yet to be invented, and no recycling for the busy housewife to be concerned about. Collections were always weekly with the binman hoisting the bin on his back and carried to the truck. No doubt not a few retired early, suffering from back problems.

No supermarkets as we now know them, though most towns possessed a 'Woollies' (Woolworths) for just about everything – and sweets, lots of them. Generally speaking, we ate healthily and were all of a normal build apart from my mother. She was well pro-portioned, leading on one occasion to being the butt of a cruel joke.

One day, we were all in the car on a family outing, I forget to where. A comment was made about my dear mothers' waistline, not for the first time. She was a bit narked about this and angrily admonished us:

'I really think that joke is wearing a bit thin.'

An unfortunate choice of words. In reply, quick as a flash, we children in the back seat piped up with, 'Still as fat as ever!' Unkind.

Time was always found for baking a cake, which reminds me of our juvenile sense of humour:

'Mummy, please can I lick the bowl out?'

'No, pull the chain like everybody else.'

Rationing

Food rationing and frugality; a way of life. How often we heard the expression:

'Look after the pennies and the pounds will look after themselves.'

For many years after the war, housewives were still using ration books, containing coupons for a variety of items. It was essential to manage these coupons prudently. Fortunately, food rationing was lifted gradually on various products throughout the early 1950s.

For a nation of tea drinkers, the end of tea rationing in 1952 was particularly welcomed, with the result that tea leaves no longer needed to be re-used. Tea bags were a rarity but even when they became more readily available, were considered by many to make an inferior cup of tea. This view might still prevail with the occasional diehard.

Fuel was rationed until 1950. Of special benefit to me as a small boy was the end of sweet rationing in 1953. Finally, meat came off ration in 1954 and although the average family was unable to afford meat every day, priority was always given to the Sunday roast.

Fuel rationing was reintroduced briefly in 1956 at the time of the Suez Crisis; very nearly again in 1973 as a result of the oil embargo imposed by OPEC on countries that supported Israel during the Yom Kippur conflict. Oil prices quadrupled, ration books were issued for all car owners, but in the event not used. But I still have mine. I am a bit of a hoarder: I am still holding on to my 1940s Under-Sixteen-Years Identity Card.

Mealtimes

Our parents insisted we ate supper together, as a family. For this rule ever to be broken the circumstances needed to be exceptional. To eat a meal in front of the television was unthinkable. At mealtimes, Dad noticed when we were very young, we ate our favourite element of the meal first, then when older the least favourite first 'to get it out of the way'. It was not until older still did we eat the meal in the accustomed way. I expect many little people behave in similar fashion today.

We were expected to hold and use our cutlery correctly, English style (much less in evidence today with American habits becoming prevalent) and to eat all the food placed in front of us. To lick our knife was an absolute taboo. Quite right too, but this habit too is seen with increasing frequency in eating establishments.

I was content with the food placed in front of me, I never considered whether there might be an alternative. My sister was a different matter, a very fussy eater. This infuriated our mother as she couldn't bear to see food wasted, having lived through the Second World War. To say she attempted to force-feed poor Sue might not be a great exaggeration.

My sister Sue

My dear sister, now departed from this world, was rebellious, a tomboy and a constant trial for our parents, but I loved her dearly and miss her greatly. In an attempt to tame her, she was given a convent education. This backfired somewhat as there is nothing more wayward than a convent schoolgirl when away from the discipline and stern gaze of Mother Superior.

There is no question that, for whatever reason, Sue was a naughty girl. My exasperated parents eventually, with some embarrassment, sought outside help but nothing was going to much change my sister.

She was undoubtedly intelligent but perhaps because she didn't pay attention at school, homework became a constant problem. I found to my surprise I was moderately successful in helping her, so much so that I wondered whether teaching could be my vocation. Dad replied:

'Maybe, but with your grasp of finance, banking might be more the career for you.'

I think this comment was based on the simple fact that I was careful with my pocket money: I had no choice, there was so little of it I had to make it last.

As an aside on the subject of careers, in my early years I did give some thought to what I would like to do when grown up. (I never had a vocation to become a doctor, whatever I might have said at my Eleven-Plus interview.) I considered the Met Office, given my interest in the weather, the Forestry Commission as I loved being outdoors, even a construction company, either John Laing or Tarmac, as I was aware the country was embarking on building a network of motorways across the country. I also had other ideas. I once said to Dad:

'I want to be an actor.'

'No you don't', he replied.

Unlike me, Sue was blessed with perfect sight, not surprising she didn't bear my affliction when it is remembered she was adopted. But like me, she suffered from a poor set of teeth, worse than mine in fact, necessitating several visits to a London Dental Hospital. She was taken up for each appointment by Mum, or occasionally Dad, and during school holidays I sometimes joined them for the daytrip. Little improvement was achieved though, with Sue remaining in poor dental health until the day she died.

Sue enjoyed a love of horses, taking every opportunity to ride. Mum arranged rides for her at a local pony club and later at a farm during family holidays in Wales. She rode with 'a good posture' according to mother, not a description she gave *me* the one time I tried it out. Sue dreamt of having a pony of her own, but family finances meant this wasn't going to happen. The purchase cost of a pony was not a major problem, more the running costs.

Dancing – another love of Sue's. Mum took her to her weekly class in Trowbridge which coincided nicely with our mothers' dog training session on the same night. For a brief time, Sue attended ballet classes but soon lost interest – no boys there.

Mum and Sue suffered a difficult relationship with constant rows about her behaviour and her insolence. I accept she was a difficult child but my mother did not always treat her with the love and respect she deserved.

After an unhappy childhood, Sue left home, just 16-years-old. I had moved out the previous year as a 17-year-old, into my first bedsit. Quite a different scenario to today when children often continue to live at home well into their twenties and sometimes beyond.

My brother Tony – his early days

Tony died at the tragically young age of 29 years from cancer, but he packed a lot of life into those years. He experienced a tempestuous relationship with our mother, nonetheless he loved her dearly as she loved him. Was he her favourite? Possibly, but if so, this didn't faze me, such matters are as they are. Flaming rows between them were a regular occurrence. I wished for no part in these, leaving them to it, slinking off to my bedroom at the first sign of an impending scene.

Tony was academically gifted, top of the form and popular with school staff. He spent time after school in the science laboratory, assisted by his chemistry master. For this he was bullied by his classmates with unpleasant slogans scribbled on his possessions, including his gym trainers ('daps' in Wiltshire speak).

He studied French and gained a notably high mark in his GCE examination, no doubt helped in no small part by his French exchange with Jacque. While Jacque was staying with us, I tried out some of my limited schoolboy French on him: much embarrassment on my part. I was not offered a French exchange but then I showed no aptitude in the subject.

Outwardly, Tony appeared an upright, honest citizen and generally speaking he was, nevertheless he was not immune from trying his hand at a little petty shop-lifting when young. This entailed rarely more than the occasional packet of sweets. Was this to curry favour with his bullying classmates? Once, more seriously, he stole a bedside alarm clock.

Very soon after this episode, word reached our parents through a report in the *Wiltshire Gazette* that a spate of local shop-lifting had been unearthed. Tony was worried, frightened he was going to be found out. I witnessed him making scratch marks on the clock, so should it be discovered he would claim he found it by the roadside. That scare marked the end of his dabble in shop-lifting and other varied misdemeanours.

More on Tony later.

Christmas

Come December, we all looked forward to Christmas, not for the mass commercialisation and excess of presents seen today, but for the thought of two full weeks off school – and excited by any talk of a White Christmas. In Wiltshire, we were treated to this delight just once throughout the 1950s – in 1959 – but another year it did snow heavily on Boxing Day.

Tangerines appearing at the greengrocer was a topic of conversation at school, this being a sign the holiday was not too far away. The fruit was full of pips yet we were very happy to cope with that, much easier to peel than oranges.

During the winter term I saved pocket money for a special cause. Close to the last day of term I visited my favourite sweet shop in Melksham to spend around ten shillings (50p) on a selection of goodies to stock up my sweet store. I must have irritated the shop owner with my requests for a few pennies-worth of this and tuppence-worth of that, but she showed no apparent annoyance. I don't know why I didn't just make my choices from Woolworth's Pick-'n-Mix counter, introduced in 1958.

A few days before Christmas, never earlier, we created and arranged our homemade decorations, but in common with most of our neighbours rarely bought a tree. Christmas itself was a meagre affair, there just wasn't the money. We received a stocking from Father Christmas with a tangerine safely stored in the toe, together with a few modest gifts.

Being brought up in a house full of dogs led me to an avid interest in all the different breeds. I was once given a copy of *The Observer's Book of Dogs*, soon learning to recognise every breed of dog in the book. A treasured gift: I still have it somewhere. On another occasion I received a bowlful of goldfish, not of great interest to me and they all died before I returned to school in January.

Each year I looked forward to a fresh supply of coloured Plasticine, a soft type of play clay, still available today, albeit Play-Doh is now far more popular. I spent many happy hours moulding Plasticine into a variety of unidentifiable shapes. Not a lot else in my stocking although I was every year the happy recipient of a Cadbury's Selection Box. Oh joy!

NB: Plasticine – much later remembered by The Beatles in a line from *Lucy in the Sky with Diamonds*

– 'Plasticine porters with looking glass ties.' (I believed the line ended with glass *eyes* until I looked it up).

One year I pleaded with my parents for a proper cowboy outfit. I already owned my cap gun but that was the sum total of my get-up. They gave me the usual 'wait and see' which raised my hopes considerably. The big day arrived. Rapidly I tore open the parcel to be greeted with – oh no! – just a cowboy holster, simply a belt with a leather pocket attached to hold my cap gun. My parents saw my disappointment and to pacify me said they could add to the outfit each birthday and Christmas, with the words:

'Just be patient.' But the rest never arrived.

Unlike a well-heeled friend, I was never the lucky recipient of a toy pedal car, my numerous requests being ignored. I would have loved to ride this around the garden. Instead, and not quite the same thing, from presents and pocket money I collected *Dinky* cars and similar vehicles. Just a thought – I am sure it was something to do with playing with the pride of my collection, an articulated lorry, that helped me in later life successfully reverse a caravan. It's all a question of knowing which way to turn the steering wheel – and crucially, by how much.

Many boys collected and played with toy soldiers which regularly featured on Christmas wish lists. This hobby didn't interest me but Tony was exceptionally proud of his collection. He was also a keen Meccano engineer. I wasn't allowed or invited to play with this until he lost interest and passed the collection to me.

Then there was Tony's butterfly collection and at Christmas he asked for books on the subject. During the summer months, he was often spotted running through the fields waving his net, while carrying other essential equipment. He built a very impressive glass cabinet to display his trophies; a talented brother.

Butterflies are not so plentiful today, I fear.

Our parents were regular church-goers, we all were then, particularly Midnight Mass on Christmas Eve. In 1957 Lonnie Donegan released a classic, *'Puttin' on the Style'*, the opening lines of Lonnie's version being:

> *Sweet Sixteen, goes to church, just to see the boys,*
> *Laughs and screams and giggles at every little noise*

Dad heard this while I was listening to Radio Luxembourg one night: he thought the lyrics to be blasphemous, offensive and in very bad taste. He was a bit like that.

Despite money being in short supply, Mum always laid on a feast for our Christmas dinner, saving throughout the year to ensure funds were available for a large turkey with all the trimmings, even if it meant going short elsewhere. I thoroughly enjoyed the meal, provided I was given plenty of my favourite ingredient – crispy roast potatoes. My grandmother joined us each year making the meal a truly family affair.

It was a house rule that after Christmas dinner (and on those Sundays when fortunate to enjoy a roast dinner), Tony was nominated to do the washing-up, I was assigned to dry the dishes and Sue was tasked with putting everything away.

Communication

No mobile phones in the 1950s, nevertheless we managed to keep in touch with family and friends. We benefited from an efficient, reliable postal service with two daily deliveries. A letter posted by 6.00 pm invariably arrived at its destination early the following morning. There was no such thing as first and second-class mail, it was all first class. In towns and cities, with several daily deliveries, a letter posted early morning would likely arrive later that afternoon.

Much excitement was generated when telephone cables were installed in our road and we became the proud owners of our first landline telephone. Quite a leap into technology but not perfect – our line was destined to be a shared line with our neighbours, the arrangement known as a 'party line'. It was possible to listen in on our neighbours' telephone conversations, should we be so inclined.

When the line was free, that is when not in use by our neighbours, nor hogged by my mother, I took the opportunity to phone Philip for a natter. Ok, I would then be hogging the phone. One pastime was for us both to place the handsets on our respective floors and shout down the line from the opposite side of our rooms, to determine if we could hear each other. Simple pleasures.

Telephones comprised a circular dial, one numerical digit to be dialled at a time, the quickest number to dial being '1', the slowest '9'. We were told about the emergency line, 999.

'Why 999, Dad, it's quicker to dial 111, surely?'

'The number is 999, don't ask me why.'

There was sense in my reasoned argument: some other countries adopted 111 as the emergency number, although now with digital telephones the question is immaterial.

Sylvia

For a few years in the 1950s, my parents fostered a teenage girl, Sylvia. I don't remember how this came about but I have fond memories of her. She was a girl who liked to live life to the full. And so she did.

Just a short distance up the road from our house in Spa Road was Melksham RAF Station, not an airport with a runway but a technical training college for RAF personnel. In the early 1940s, it also became a base for visiting American infantry as part of the build-up of American troops in Wiltshire and elsewhere. An American presence was maintained after the war and Sylvia, being Sylvia, was a regular visitor at the station. Before long she married a First Lieutenant and emigrated to Brooklyn, New York.

I visited Sylvia when on a work secondment in New York in 1986. I found her still living in Brooklyn, now with a very young second husband, Moises, a gold-digging Egyptian. I met up a few times with Sylvia, occasionally with the Egyptian, during my few weeks in the city before my return to the UK. Sylvia was still innocent in many ways, but Moises was calculating, smarmy and hard to like – although Sylvia adored him. Sadly, Sylvia died not long after my visit, struck down by a return of breast cancer. Which worked out well for Moises.

Television

I earlier briefly mentioned television. In 1953 we purchased our first set, a 12″ model, specifically to watch the Queen's Coronation (of more later) and a BBC 'H' type roof aerial was erected. Shortly after the TV purchase, a free-standing glass magnifying screen was purchased and placed in front of the set. This increased marginally the size of the picture but required sitting immediately in front of the television to see anything. Family members (like me) sitting only slightly to one side saw very little. We soon discarded the magnifier, more trouble than it was worth.

The grainy black and white picture was not all that bad until the horizontal hold started playing up, the picture moving slowly up or down the screen; a regular occurrence. Dad fiddled with the controls to steady the image, which was fine until the picture started travelling in the opposite direction, or the vertical hold had a go at trying his patience. Ah, we don't have nearly so much fun today with our digital televisions.

Until some years ago, television sets were built around a cathode ray tube which created a shape similar to a square cardboard box, hence for years to come the TV was called 'The Box', and not just by us: the expression became in use country-wide.

Sets were sometimes enclosed within a wooden cabinet with optional doors on the front, making it look even more like a box.

Those early televisions, with the screen using a 405-lines format, created a glare that was considered by some to be bad for the eyes, particularly if the viewer was sitting close to the set (which was a necessity due to the small screen). The resolution was later increased to 625-lines which was an improvement but still a far cry compared with modern sets.

Dixon of Dock Green, starring Jack Warner, became a firm family favourite on Saturday evenings; such simple, innocent days. A weekly treat was watching Dixon with a plateful of marmite on toast – using Mother's Pride bread, of course. The show represented the 'Bobby on the Beat', a rare sight nowadays. *Hancock's Half Hour*, now moved from radio to TV, was not to be missed. *Reluctant Heroes* with Brian Rix, a televised film based on the stage play – at the time hilarious – and *Whack-O!* starring Jimmy Edwards, both essential viewing then, but so dated today.

Another dated programme was *Circus Boy*, a loud American TV series starring Micky Dolenz, later to find fame as the drummer in The Monkees. Dad thought this American export to be particularly bad; in retrospect, I agree.

If our parents were busy and one of us fancied watching a particular television programme, Dad would always ask:

'Is it educational?'

We sometimes persuaded him to believe it was indeed so, but we never tried to convince him that the likes of *Circus Boy* would do wonders for our education.

For something scary I was allowed, surprisingly, to watch *Quatermass and the Pit*, even though I was young and no doubt at an impressionable age. But I survived, without nightmares.

September 1955 heralded the first ITV broadcast but it was to be a couple of years before we managed to persuade Dad to invest in a new TV and aerial, thereby giving us a choice – two TV channels! This led to the oft-quoted question when bored with the current offering: 'What's on the other side?' Programmes had to be watched when transmitted, otherwise never, this being long before video recorders or 'catch-up'.

To watch both BBC and ITV, we invested in a new 14″ black-and-white TV and the required new aerial, then much excitement while we waited for the new aerial to be fitted. Installation dates were agreed, then cancelled, but finally, it was all systems go. Except it wasn't. To our dismay, the new TV couldn't be tuned to the new aerial; much disappointment all round.

Eventually with the problem finally fixed, we were able to watch ITV: *Double Your Money* with Hughie Green became a favourite. I rarely missed *Take Your Pick!* with Michael Miles, the best bit for me being the *Yes-No Interlude*. So hard to say neither 'yes' nor 'no', under a barrage of questions from the host. Tony and I watched *The Benny Hill*

101

Show, risqué for its day, though at the time I doubt I understood all his smutty jokes. Dad hated it.

We loved ITV adverts: *'You'll Wonder Where the Yellow Went…'*, *'Fry's Turkish Delight'*, both adverts with a catchy theme tune; *'Go to Work on an Egg'*, unsurprisingly sponsored by the Egg Marketing Board, and *'Happiness is a Cigar called Hamlet'*. No restrictions on advertising tobacco, or alcohol, in those early commercial TV days.

The Independent Television Authority limits how much time is allowed for adverts. For many years this was set at 8 minutes per hour, increased much later to the current level of 12 minutes, albeit with some restrictions. Not many people know that.

On Saturday afternoons ITV broadcast World Wrestling, of no interest to us but visiting a friend one Saturday, I saw his dad watching the spectacle. Fake or what! His dad was an avid viewer, believing it all to be genuine stuff. This 'sport' disappeared from television for a while, although I believe is again available on a minority TV channel.

Towards the end of the 1950s we were treated to exciting live TV pop music shows, the likes of which had not been seen before. *Six-Five Special* (BBC) always shown at five past six on Saturday evenings, ran from 1957 to 1958, and *Oh Boy!* (ITV) from 1958-59. Then *Juke Box Jury* (BBC), a pop music panel show that ran from 1959 until 1967 (with later revivals). *Top of the Pops* (BBC), probably the longest-running TV show of its genre, was not to appear until 1964.

The Eurovision Song Contest was first held in 1956, in those days broadcast in black and white. In the early years the United Kingdom ('Royaume-Uni') enjoyed success with several respectable results. Not so today.

It was to be many years, well into the 1960s, before such shows could be appreciated in the UK on a colour television. And flat-screen televisions were generations away, not even a dream in the 1950s.

Hobbies

Pocket money – my initial allowance, before modest annual increases, amounted to 2/- (10p) a week. For a while, I found that if I asked Mum, then separately Dad, for my pocket money, I gained a total of four shillings. This 'scam' worked well until ultimately my ruse was discovered.

I was given a pay rise each birthday but this never amounted to very much. On the plus side, having minimal pocket money did help instil in me a work ethic. From the age of 13 years, by asking around, I obtained various part-time employments during school holidays.

Pop music – I was keen on most genres of music from an early age, particularly pop music. With my pocket money and irregular earnings, I bought, and avidly read, the pop magazines of the day: *New Musical Express*, (still around today as *NME*), *Melody Maker,* and occasionally *Disc.*

My first 7" 45rpm record purchase was in 1958 – *'Hoots Mon'* by Lord Rockingham's Eleven. I rarely purchased new records, most bought either from a second-hand record shop in Trowbridge, or market stalls.

In the early days of my collecting I didn't have a record player, consequently the collection was of only limited use (I read the labels) but after incessantly badgering my parents they presented me with a magnificent birthday gift, one of my all-time favourite presents, a Dansette record player – complete with 9-disc auto-change! I was thrilled, absolutely delighted.

The hobby didn't end in the 1950s. By the end of the 1970s I possessed a collection of well over 600 singles.

Pets - when not at school, watching TV or playing records on my new record player, I was developing further hobbies. For a short while I kept white mice, not for long as they came with a nasty habit of biting me. I owned two budgerigars, given to me as a birthday present. They were short-lived too as I soon lost interest, finding them quite boring pets.

After the mice and budgerigars, it was third time lucky, finding success breeding chinchilla rabbits to raise much-needed funds; I become something of an entrepreneur. I bred several litters each year (they bred like, well, like rabbits).

I learnt essential skills such as not to handle the baby bunnies ('kits'), until at least 7 days old, any earlier they faced being killed by the doe when placed back in the hutch. She was funny like that. A heavy thunderstorm once broke soon after a litter was born and to my distress, I found the little dead bodies the following morning. Just as well for my business that they were so easy to breed. The hobby was quite an earner, I usually managed to sell each kit for 2/6d (12½p).

I cleaned out the hutches most weekends, disinfecting with DDT (a very effective but long-banned substance) to control the ants and other infestations. The hobby kept me amused for a couple of years until one day my parents' dogs broke into the hutches and slaughtered the lot.

Photography – a hobby in which all family members took an active interest. As paying for developing and printing was relatively expensive, my mother invested in all the necessary equipment to do the job herself (black and white prints, of course). A room in the cottage was set aside as her darkroom: I can still remember the smell of the fluids used in the procedure. Not nice.

During holidays I advanced my own interest in photography. Mum bought me a second-hand Box Brownie camera which became my pride and joy. To this day I have held on to my better photographic efforts, but sadly not the Box Brownie itself, now a collector's item.

Later, mother invested in an 8mm cine camera which caused much excitement as it filmed in colour! – but no sound. This was used primarily to film her menagerie of dogs although at times, much to our embarrassment, we children were filmed too. The camera was still in use much later to film the weddings of myself, my sister and brother.

Other hobbies – with my brother I shared an electric train set, briefly mentioned earlier. This was made by Trix, we were not fans of Hornby. Hardly 'a set' at the outset, but over time with our pocket money and other earnings we built up an acceptable collection.

Later on, Tony developed other interests and the train set passed to me. I set it up on my bedroom floor. I liked experimenting with the electrics in my attempts to make the trains go faster, but this resulted in a little accident. For some reason, the cables from the transformer to the track started smouldering, causing burn marks across the bedroom carpet. I was horrified. Thinking quickly,

I moved my bed to cover the burn marks, rearranging the remaining furniture. It did not take long for Mum to notice the reorganisation of my room and she asked me what I thought I was doing:

'I just fancied a change,' I lied, hoping she believed the innocent face I was trying to maintain. I got away with it. For a while.

Catapults – I never owned such a weapon although some boys brought them, illegally, into school, risking punishment. But I made a bow and arrow set, not very successfully, nor did I make an effective marksman. Once I accidentally hit one of the dogs, she made a lot of noise but I found no sign of injury. I thought better of asking Mum to have a look at the unfortunate animal.

More sedentary hobbies included collecting cigarette cards, cigarette packets, stamps – both UK and abroad. A cherished collection was beer bottle tops from the supplies Dad brought home regularly from the off-licence. I sold the rusty collection in 2008 to an avid collector in Finland for £75. He seemed happy, giving me a five-star review on eBay. It takes all sorts.

Radio fascinated me, in some ways more so than television and not just because it was only on radio that Tony and I could listen secretly (we were quite young at the time) to *Journey into Space* once in bed and the light switched off. This was a science fiction programme, each 30-minute episode opening with a haunting reading of the shows' title, followed by a scary music track. A typical plot line:

The year is 1965 and Jet launches his A.24 rocket from the Rocket Research Station at Poker Flats. But something goes wrong, and the rocket heads towards Las Vegas, out of control…

We loved the radio programmes of the time, *Take it from Here* starring Jimmy Edwards, June Whitfield and others. Every episode featured an episode from 'The Glums', a long-engaged couple, Ron and Eth. Very funny.

We listened avidly to the truly wonderful Radio Luxembourg broadcasting on 208 metres medium waveband, reception was often dreadful but the music was excellent.

On the station we listened to pop music interspersed with adverts, including Jimmy Savile no less, seeking members for his 'Teen and Twenty Disc Club'. I joined. We heard continuous adverts from Horace Batchelor of Keynsham ('spelt K, E, Y…) who claimed his 'Infra-Draw Method' on the 'Treble Chance' would win you good money on the football pools. His advertisement can still be heard on YouTube. We did wonder if he was so good at predictions, why he didn't just keep quiet and play the pools for himself.

A popular BBC radio programme, *Down Your Way*, ran from 1946 until 1992, transmitted on the Home Service (now Radio 4). This was a roadshow which travelled to towns around the United Kingdom, interviewing notable local residents and dignitaries, then playing their choice of music. As Dad managed a large business in Devizes, second only to Wadworth's Brewery, he was approached to participate. This created much excitement at home. Unfortunately, he was not selected to take part, the reason given by the producer of the programme being:

'Sorry, Mr Walker, but you don't sound local enough.'

This was Wiltshire, the BBC expecting everyone to speak in the local dialect.

I built a crystal radio set with Dad's help; well in truth, he built it. This was not a great success with reception almost non-existent. Intermittently I tuned in successfully to just one unknown station, eventually giving up in frustration, graduating to listening to short wave radio stations on an old large valve-operated family wireless.

I brought this grand receiver back into use during the 1960s, listening to pirate radio. The set displayed twelve mechanical buttons for storing pre-tuned stations: I found a pirate station for each button.

From 1923 until the early 1990s, it was BBC radio that broadcast SOS personal messages, often just before News bulletins. As an example, these read along lines similar to the following:

Would Mrs Joan Walker, believed to be on holiday in Dorset, please contact Bristol Royal Infirmary where her mother is seriously ill.

We wondered how often these messages reached the intended recipient. Now, with the widespread use of mobile phones, there is little need for the service.

Reading - I read a little for pleasure as a break from school text books. At my final school Speech Day, I was presented with my GCE certificate together with a prize for passing my exams – a book of H G Wells short stories which I thoroughly enjoyed. Sadly, I have lost the book. This was about the extent of my serious reading apart from novels by Sir Arthur Conan Doyle and those well-worn pages from *Lady Chatterley's Lover* (of course I read those, I was a schoolboy).

But my reading was just as likely to be comics, at primary school the *Swift*, at secondary school progressing to the *Eagle*. I was not allowed *Beano* or *Dandy* ('undesirable' says my father) although these were brought into school by other boys for us all to share. The *Eagle* Annual was a much-cherished Christmas present by those lucky enough to receive one.

Gardening – in the summer months I mowed the large lawn – for payment. Not exactly a hobby but the task kept me occupied. I earned every penny, struggling with that heavy Qualcast push-mower. I helped Dad weed the garden and for all my gardening chores was paid a shilling (5p) an hour. An hour was all I usually lasted before boredom and/or tiredness intervened. I preferred walking the dogs to all that, happy to do so without payment. I was an outdoor child.

A little flutter

Dad's job and his never-ending work on the cottage left little time for hobbies, but he did fill in religiously his 'Treble Chance' football coupon every Wednesday evening. Apart from the odd five bob (25p) win, he was invariably unsuccessful. I mentioned Horace Batchelor:

'No way. I've heard of him, it's a con.'

Occasionally, Mum and Dad attended Point-to-Point amateur horse racing meetings. I would be left

111

at home with Tony, but one weekend they took me along. They explained the betting procedure and why, on the first race on the card, they were placing bets on two particular horses. I liked the name of another horse and suggested they put a bet on for me. They gave me a withering look as if to say, 'You know nothing.'

The race started with the shout 'They're off!' (nowadays I hear the expression 'They're racing!'). My parents lost both their bets. 'My' horse won. So there.

This beginner's luck (although a bet hadn't, of course, been placed) gave me a taste for horse racing, or rather sporadic betting. Over the years I have been reasonably successful with my annual bet on the Aintree Grand National. I also bet annually on the Epsom Derby, but to date have lost every bet on that particular race.

Dogs and cats

Mum bred dogs – dachshunds (sausage dogs) and miniature poodles. This sometimes-profitable hobby was registered with Crufts as 'Bowerhill Kennels', the name taken from a nearby suburb of Melksham. She won Best of Breed with a wire-haired dachshund at Crufts. She won a Best of Breed again at another championship show with a miniature poodle, full of character, bizarrely named

'Mr Brown'. This dog was headhunted by a breeder in the USA who gave my mother an unbelievable offer for the unfortunate animal which was carted off – in a crate – and flown to his new owner in the States. Some dogs were pets, others were strictly business and for breeding.

Dachshunds need no clipping but poodles most certainly do. In addition to dog breeding, my mother helped make ends meet with poodle clipping (or 'pruning', as I prefer to call it) for which she possessed a remarkable talent. Nowadays poodle wool has monetary value and is in demand to be crafted or knitted into various accessories. When I think of all that poodle wool just chucked in the bin…

Again to raise funds, Mum boarded dogs, accepting any variety. This brought money into the household but subjected us to various downsides, not least the incessant barking throughout the night by the anxious dogs, keeping us all awake.

I grew up with dachshunds and poodles, though it is the dachshunds I remember, a remarkable breed in some ways, fiercely loyal, intelligent, sometimes noisy. I don't know if they were originally bred for routing rabbits out of burrows, but this was for them a favourite pastime.

An incident is remembered for the three days one pet dachshund disappeared. On the third day it was found, or rather heard yapping, down a rabbit hole, presumably unable to move neither forward nor by reversing out. During that third day the unfortunate canine was encouraged to wriggle out, having lost sufficient weight to escape. Thereafter, dachshunds were kept firmly on leads if in rabbit territory.

Much of my exercise came from walking the dogs across the local fields, down to the canal, the river and elsewhere. I loved the exploring that came with this, always happy to respond to my mothers' frequent request:

'Be a dear, Chrissy, give the dogs a run.'

At the end of a rare family summer holiday in Cornwall, in 1958, a local farmer gave me a ginger kitten, female I was told, unusual for a ginger cat. I named her Puddy. She was affectionate with a sweet nature towards humans, yet teased mercilessly the family dogs. They gave chase daily but never caught Puddy. She became a very dear pet for several years until she suffered a sudden and fatal heart attack. A sad day.

For a while, Mum dabbled in breeding Siamese cats. Intelligent and independent (like most cats), I was once involved, personally. Late one evening we watched a very heavily pregnant queen pacing the floors, certainly looking for a place to give birth. A purpose-built quiet area was provided but she didn't seem interested in that. Mother commented,

'In the morning, we'll find out just where she decided to deliver.'

I slept well that night, at least until the early hours when I was woken by the sound of relentless meowing. The cat had decided that the warmest, darkest, quietest place for her purpose was at the foot of my bed – and inside my bed.

I woke Mum, well, I thought I ought to. She retrieved the mother and her kittens, changed my bedding and let me get back to sleep.

All four kittens survived their ordeal.

8

OUT AND ABOUT

Sweets – and the dentist

During school holidays I sometimes caught the bus into Devizes to visit the renowned Thursday market, held in the main square – the same square to be used later for filming 'Far from the Madding Crowd', the 1967 version starring the schoolboys' desire, Julie Christie. This was a massive market – and still is today, still held on Thursdays. The attraction for me was the array of sweet stalls selling large variety packs of confectionery, noticeably cheaper than in the sweet shops in Trowbridge.

To buy propriety varieties of sweets – my favourites included Trebor sherbet dip, Spangles, flying saucers and sweet cigarettes – involved a trip to the sweet shop where, in addition to these delights, I would be tempted to buy loose sweets from the vast array of jars – pineapple chunks and sherbet lemons to mention just two; never aniseed drops which I seriously disliked and still do.

I wasn't allowed bubble gum nor chewing gum but I wasn't keen on bubble-gum anyway so that wasn't a problem. I occasionally bought Wrigley's Spearmint Gum but never chewing the product at home. I was not in the habit of looking for trouble.

If flush with pocket money (a rare occurrence) I bought a Burton's Wagon Wheel, still available today — did they ever go away? – now a little smaller, I think. Or is it just that I am bigger now?

This captivation with sweets did not help the health of my teeth. I should have realised the error of my ways when an appointment with a dentist revealed no fewer than seven cavities to be filled and two teeth to be extracted. The work was not to be carried out in entirety on the same day, thankfully: a series of appointments was made. Or perhaps not so thankfully, better to have all the pain handled in a single day?

No modern high-speed drill, just the slow, grinding mechanism hanging over me. Oh yes, I remember it well: the noise, the vibration and of course the pain. On one of the appointments it became necessary for the dental nurse to physically restrain me while the dentist carried out his evil work.

Probably due in no small part to my addiction in my youth to sweets, I have long been the bearer of a poor set of teeth, in addition to my inherited short-sightedness. Also, during the 1960s my hearing was affected by listening to far too much loud music, which has left me in my dotage with increasing deafness. Still, no worries, must look on the bright side.

Cinema

Trowbridge cinema was a continual attraction. We sat in the 1/9d's (8p), the 2/6d's (12½p) too great a strain on our meagre pocket money. In those days a feature film was shown together with a 'B' movie (sometimes better than the main attraction). And Pathe News.

With friends, I saw many a good film there: *The Bridge on the River Kwai,* the 1957 film with Alec Guinness and Jack Hawkins, and *Dunkirk* (the 1958 version), an educational and moving film. For lighter relief we watched *Blue Murder at St. Trinians, 20,000 Leagues under the Sea,* and the Cliff Richard film *Expresso Bongo* – an 'A' classification owing to the brief glimpse of a female breast. With that films' rating, I should have been accompanied by an adult. How things have changed.

The evenings always ended with the National Anthem.

The mid-1950s saw the emergence of Rock 'n' Roll – Elvis Presley, Gene Vincent, Eddie Cochran and the rest – and Bill Haley and his Comets. Bill's film, *Rock Around the Clock,* led to riots in cinemas across the country, including ripping upholstery from cinema seats. I watched the film at Trowbridge but was disappointed not to witness any rioting – just raucous out-of-tune singing.

In 1961 (ok, not the 1950s, but included here while I'm on the subject of cinema), on my sixteenth birthday I met up with David, my close friend from secondary school. David was just a day older than me. We ventured into Trowbridge for our first 'X' certificate film, for which there was a requirement at that time to be at least 16-years-old. The stern lady in the ticket office turned us away, not believing we were indeed both 16-years-old.

Luckily, David's father knew the cinema manager. Once this connection was established, we were not only allowed in, but given front row seats in the circle – for free. The films, though, were something of a disappointment – *The Deadly Mantis* and *The Cyclops*. I forget which was the 'B' movie but both were equally dire and third-rate. Other films of the time such as *Saturday Night and Sunday Morning* and *A Taste of Honey,* among other 'kitchen sink' dramas, were noticeably more realistic and believable than those so-called horror films.

Childhood labour

I was fortunate as a child to enjoy a variety of activities but it all cost money, especially the smoking. Luckily for our finances we were not yet into alcohol. As soon as I reached the grand age of 14 years, to supplement my pocket money I was able to get a summer job in the local chicken processing plant. Hard work for which I earned a miserly 1/10½d (9p) an hour. Still, every little helps. Long, exhausting days, with the shift often not finishing until early evening – a taste of what I was to experience after my school days and into a full-time job.

A girl I knew from primary school also worked at the factory during the summer holidays. I mentioned her earlier – Carol Williams. We met up in the canteen at break time and exchanged glances of recognition, but no more. Even so, I missed her when I left the factory. Unrequited love?

My pitiful earnings kept me in sweets and buns, I was always hungry – or was it just I possessed a healthy appetite? Perhaps surprisingly, I rarely put on weight. It is a different story today.

I was later to find slightly better-paid work at Swanage, but it was still going to be hard graft.

More on my brother Tony

Tony, almost four years older than me, was expected to spend two years completing his National Service, but he escaped this challenge by a matter of months when the requirement ended in 1960. He was, therefore, like me, free to seek part-time work. He found summer jobs but because he did not understand the work ethic, was sacked with no notice from two jobs (no employee protection for schoolchildren). The first sacking was for insubordination, the second for reading a newspaper when his eyes should have been glued to monitoring machinery to ensure it was operating safely and not risking the lives of the operators.

Other jobs he tried were met with more success. During various vacations he found temporary employment at Usher's Brewery in Trowbridge; with a popular chain of steak restaurants in Bristol (Berni Inns); and in summer, catering in a large hotel in Swanage. Each December, with other students, he worked at the Post Office sorting Christmas cards.

Later, Tony applied for a place at Oxford University. He was offered an interview and a second, but unfortunately no place. Disappointed, he applied to Bristol University, received an invitation to interview and this time was offered a place.

This was not to last as he enjoyed student life in Bristol immensely and to the full, too much so, being sent down after two years, still having problems with the principles of work. It was then to Manchester University where he knew it was imperative to knuckle down and study. And study he did. He obtained a degree in biochemistry but his short career was to be with an early computer company. His attention was drawn in this direction as the university was playing an important role in computer development.

In Manchester he met Carole, who was later to become his wife.

9

SUMMER HOLIDAYS

An adventure in Wales

One fine summer, I joined Philip and his family for
a holiday in a cottage on the quayside at Newquay,
Wales.

After breakfast each day we set off to explore
the town. The coast path led to a hill with glorious
views over the town and sea. We climbed the hill
every day, calling it 'our mountain' although I doubt
the height amounted to much more than a couple
of hundred feet. Regularly we passed an elderly
Welsh gentleman who always greeted us with 'Good
morning, boys' in a very strong Welsh accent. This
was a new concept for us, being more used to broad
Wiltshire speak.

We wandered the narrow streets, bought sweets
and most days shared a bag of chips, even though

Philip's mother provided us with three square meals a day at the holiday cottage. We watched the fishermen on the quay, and at high tide the boats sailing in and out of the harbour. We fooled around on the beach and built impressive proper grown-up sandcastles.

We played in the harbour, at low tide climbing on a large storage box situated in the middle of the harbour, having no idea what it was or what purpose it served. We never found out. From this vantage point we watched the comings and goings on the waterfront. One memorable day we were sitting on the box chatting about nothing in particular, either unaware of the incoming spring tide or oblivious to what it meant. That is until our elderly gentleman friend called out from the quay:

'Look out boys, get out of there quick.'

We needed no persuasion once we noticed our predicament, with the sea about to lap the top of the box. It was unfortunate our observational skills were so deficient, also that we were not wearing our swimming shorts that day. We jumped into the water and half swam, half waded the thankfully short distance to the quayside and safety. We crept back to the cottage for a change of clothing and agreed not to mention the incident to Philip's parents, partly through guilt and partly through embarrassment about our general lack of awareness.

But soon our pile of wet clothes hidden in our bedroom was discovered and we had no choice but to explain our foolishness and accept a mild ticking-off. Despite that, I enjoyed an exciting and splendid week, my first holiday without my family.

A trip to Cornwall

Sadly for us both, at the end of our first year at secondary school, Philip's family moved to a cottage in Kenwyn, a village on the outskirts of Truro, Cornwall. The following summer, aged 13 years, I was again invited to spend a few days with his family, this time in Cornwall. I travelled down by train, on my own.

'You'll be fine, Christopher, a kindly lady will probably buy you a cup of tea or a glass of squash from the buffet,' my mother reassured me.

As it turned out, no refreshments for me on the journey, nevertheless I was happy, thrilled with the new experience of being allowed to travel on my own. My parents, by necessity economical, would have paid for a third-class ticket if possible, but as this class of travel was abolished a couple of years earlier, they were forced to stump up for second-class. The carriages were just the same as third-class, just renamed.

The train passed through Devon, giving me my first sight of the renowned red soil of the area, and then Dawlish, where I was excited by the sight of the sea and experiencing waves crashing over the

125

train carriage. No wonder this particular stretch of line was washed away in 2014.

Philip's family collected me from Truro station and drove to their cottage. What a delight! An old white-washed thatched cottage with a winding path leading through rose beds, down to a babbling stream at the bottom of the garden; real chocolate box stuff.

Philip was as ever in full tearaway mode. We shared a few scrapes on our trips by train into Truro to buy sweets and comics, also to Falmouth for general mucking about, including scrambling over the coastal rocks. Plenty of trains served the local vicinity, this being well before the 'Beeching Axe' of the 1960s when Dr Beeching closed many rural lines.

On our first local train outing, we thought it might be fun to pull the communication cord – 'To Stop the Train Pull Down the Chain' – but were discouraged by the next line, 'Penalty for improper use £5.'

We did misbehave on our holiday together, not always showing respect for our elders. Nevertheless, we carried out some good deeds, including clearing away a rotting lamb carcass and the remains of a rabbit from a nearby stream, both corpses rather too far gone for the cooking pot. We helped Philip's father with his gardening although I doubt we were of great assistance. We volunteered to help with the washing up, an offer taken up by his mother with genuine gratitude.

A while before my visit, Phil had acquired an old car, very old; we drove this wreck round a nearby field. The petrol tank was missing so we clipped a plastic bottle filled with petrol to the underside of the bonnet. From this we ran a plastic pipe, giving a drip feed to the carburettor. Not the safest arrangement yet with luck on our side, we survived.

One day while scrambling across seashore rocks, Phil played what I considered to be a dangerous trick on me and, without thinking, I called him the 'C' word. It took a lot to shock Philip but shocked he was by my outburst. I was used to hearing the word all the time at school, thinking it pretty harmless. He put me right, explaining in a rare serious moment for him that the word is on a totally different level of profanity to other swear words. My education was not exclusively from the teaching staff at school. That was in the 1950s. Today the word is in all too common usage and heard with increasing frequency in television dramas.

The following summer Philip travelled up to Wiltshire to spend a week with me. We visited our old haunts and now, at the ripe old age of 14 years, reminisced upon our time at primary school and our one year together at secondary school. A year after that visit I looked him up when on a family holiday in Cornwall. We continued as pen pals for a while until he moved on and we lost contact.

However, a couple of years ago I tracked Philip down, via social media, to discover life had not been kind to him. We were the very best of friends and one day I hope we will meet up again, but regrettably his name had disappeared from the internet site I revisited when compiling this book.

Swanage

It would be an unusual – and lucky – family who were able to consider a holiday abroad, package holidays to the Costa Brava and the rest still some years away. Apart from a couple of visits to other destinations, our summer family holidays were habitually on a caravan site at Swanage in Dorset, lasting for two weeks. We drove down, sometimes with a caravan on tow. Car ownership was by no means universal in the 1950s but we were fortunate in owning a car for as long as I remember. Our car was usually an old Wolseley, Dad's favourite, but in 1959 my mother bought one of the very first BMC Minis. A fun car to drive but not one for towing the caravan.

There was just one problem with these car journeys: whatever the make of car I was invariably car sick. Various medications were forced on me including *Kwells*, the family choice, but they didn't work for me. Sticks of barley sugar were helpful, sometimes. Dad was sympathetic to my plight but Mum was never happy, more than once exclaiming,

'This is impossible, we can't go *anywhere* without our journey being interrupted.'

She was not the most compassionate mother and I will relate another example later. But she was my mother and I loved her nevertheless.

It was travelling down to Swanage on one such holiday that Tony and I were faced with a pair of bullies. Parked for lunch, Mum, Dad and sister Sue ate their picnic in the caravan, while we took our packed lunches to a seat further down the layby. (I might have been car sick but that didn't put me off my food). Two charming boys appeared out of nowhere and demanded we hand over our picnics. Luckily, when Tony stood up, he appeared taller than the novice bullies realised; they skunked off.

The caravan site – This was spread over an area of disused stone quarries, with glorious views over the town of Swanage, the sea, and the Purbeck hills. The quarries are long abandoned but a little further inland Purbeck stone continues to be quarried today, enjoying a ready market.

In the early 1950s, we were the first to pitch a caravan on the site and enjoyed a good relationship with Mr Hancock, the quarry owner. An enchanted location with all the space we could desire, allowing many carefree days, happily spent playing and exploring.

One fateful day, Susan was not her usual cheerful self. To try to cheer her up, I rolled down a grassy bank, arms and legs flying, excitedly exclaiming:

'Look at me Sue, look!'

At the bottom of the slope, not spotted by me, was a barbed wire fence – my bare right leg slammed into it, becoming entangled with the barbs. My screaming was heard by Mum in the caravan some distance away but she arrived within minutes, despite her generous build, and unpicked my leg from the wire; more screaming on my part. An emergency visit to hospital followed. Another scar of which I have the remnants to this day.

Within a couple of years, the site became very popular. As visiting caravans and tents increased, dustbins were installed around the site. Every other day, Mr Hancock used his tractor and trailer to empty the bins and he allowed me to ride on the trailer, a highlight of my holiday. Great fun.

A toilet block was later built to cater for the increasing numbers of visitors and a small shop appeared on the site. In spite of the extortionate prices there, I was still tempted to buy the odd packet of sweets to tide me over until the next trip into town. The site is now a large, commercially run, operation.

The seaside – We enjoyed plenty of swimming, picnics on the beach or the Downs, sometimes with a bottle of pop, *Tizer* being a firm favourite. I was sometimes allowed to take the empty bottle back to the shop for the 2d (1p) refund – just enough to buy a 2d packet of KP peanuts.

On special occasions we were treated to fish and chips, which always taste nicer by the seaside. Why is that? Happy days.

On holiday my father continued to wear his work clothes, a suit, collared shirt and tie – in the caravan, on a walk, even on the beach; often he would wear his trilby hat. He was always well-dressed, whatever the occasion and could never be persuaded to wear shorts.

These holidays were great fun for me, my brother and my sister, but not so much fun for Dad. Although he managed to spend most weekends with the Swanage Sailing Club, he returned to Devizes, and work, very early on Monday mornings.

Caravans lettings – Our mother, over time, bought three fairly dilapidated caravans, two rented out for the season and left on site all year, the third reserved for our personal use. My parents and Sue slept in this, I slept in a tent with Tony. Each weekend Mum busied herself cleaning out the rented caravans for the next visitors. Few problems were experienced with her tenants – with one notable exception. A family of particular charming tenants kindly stripped the beds and folded the sheets and blankets. On unfolding one blanket, Mum was horrified to be greeted with a surprisingly large quantity of multi-coloured vomit. Not nice.

The attraction of renting caravans diminished somewhat after this event and she sold up at the end of the season. The income from the business was most welcome in making ends meet and was sorely missed.

More bullies – During one of these Swanage holidays, I experienced my second encounter with a duo of 'not very nice boys'. I was exploring the council tip (a mountain of refuse, fascinating stuff, many a happy hour spent there rummaging) when stones were thrown at me. The boys ran off. I suffered a nasty gash just above my left eye and have a trace of the wound today, more evidence of my accident-prone early years. Should the stone have hit me just a little lower, I might have lost my sight in that eye (my 'good' eye), but I was wearing shatterproof thick glasses which probably would have saved me.

Pedalos – A special treat on holiday was to be taken out on a pedalo in Swanage Bay, Mum and Dad pedalling, Tony, Sue and myself squeezing in behind. On our first such trip – a fright for me. Our parents worked hard pedalling us out to the middle of the bay and stopped for a rest.

'Keep pedalling!' I screamed.

I was sure we would sink if the craft stopped moving. It took some time before realisation dawned – we were not, in fact, about to be submerged. A few years ago on a return visit to Swanage, I hired a pedalo and was reminded just how scared I had been that day.

I was, though, happy and unconcerned on paddle-steamer day trips to Bournemouth on the *PS Monarch*. That vessel is no more but *PS Waverley*, the last ocean-going paddle-steamer in the world, continued to make her annual pilgrimage to Swanage until 2018; the future is looking a little uncertain.

A job – Swanage gave me another opportunity to earn a bit of extra cash to supplement my pocket money. For two summers I found casual work washing-up at Swanage Ocean Bay café (now a posh restaurant), earning 2/6d (12½p) per hour – a welcome increase on my abysmal rate of pay at the chicken processing plant. The café was not particularly inspiring work and, as the boss was a most objectionable fellow with an alarming temper, I searched the town for alternative employment. Nothing else filled me with much enthusiasm; I stayed with the washing-up.

In town – We all had our bikes, me on my sturdy but ancient Rudge (worth good money today). We cycled around the site and into town for the beach, funfair and amusement arcades. Glorious summer days.

The funfair included dodgems (known to us then as bumper cars) right on the seafront. The attraction is now long gone, the site today being a garish amusement arcade filled with an array of slot machines and 'Penny Falls'. Addictive for some. Candy floss was always available but I was not keen on that, quite surprising really, considering my sweet tooth.

On the beach, Punch and Judy but no donkey rides, I know not why. Shops in the town displayed racks of saucy postcards, saucy then but rather tame today. I did start a collection of the 'better' cards, to which I have since added, now owning a sizeable and colourful collection.

Kitty – We delayed our departure on one Swanage holiday as the latest family cat, Kitty (ok, not a very original name) disappeared, just as we were about to deliver her to the cattery. Perhaps she knew. We searched far and wide, high and low, calling for her, 'Here Kitty Kitty, here Kitty Kitty' all to no avail. After much discussion we decided to leave for Swanage as two caravans were waiting to be cleaned for tenants arriving later that day. We asked our neighbours to keep a look-out and to telephone the campsite manager should she turn up.

The caravan was hooked-up and we were on our way, looking forward to the holiday but now with heavy heart. We eventually arrived on site and started to unpack. From underneath the bunk beds, out sprung Kitty.

A girl – My parents became friends with other happy campers and caravanners on the site. One such family was the Schmidt's, who coincidentally also lived in Melksham, with their young attractive daughter, Hannah. One year, it must have been around 1956 or 1957, a travelling funfair came to town. We paid a visit.

The parents were not keen on the big wheel but thought it a great idea for Hannah and myself to have a go. Hannah was all for it, but this meant me sharing a seat in close proximity to a girl. With my enduring shyness this was not an activity I welcomed, but with reluctance I took my seat next to Hannah, much embarrassment on my part. If the occasion had occurred a couple of years later, I might have relished the opportunity.

The tub – My father owned a sizeable sailing dinghy, a heavy T-class, registration T100, constructed with oak and a complete absence of any lightweight materials. The boat came with a tender, a small flat-bottomed dinghy we called 'The Tub'.

Many happy days I spent with Tony, rowing around Swanage Bay and to the far end of the beach

and back. These were trouble-free adventures –
until one day never to be forgotten. The weather
was warm and fine and, as always, we were enjoying
ourselves pottering about at the far end of the bay.
Eventually it was time to row our way back but, on
this occasion, the task was taking great effort
without making any apparent headway.

'Come on, Chrissy, keep rowing,' encouraged
my dear brother.

Which I did, but still no progress compared
with landmarks on the shore. We were being swept
out to sea in the general direction of the Isle of
Wight.

'Keep rowing,' Tony continued. I imagine he
took his turn on the oars although I don't remember
him doing so.

Our plight was spotted from the pier: a pleasure
boat, full of holidaymakers, was despatched to our
rescue. Once saved, we were informed by the
captain we had become trapped in a strong out-
going tide. We were reunited with our parents, not
to our mothers' relief, but for us to be met with only
harsh words:

'What were you playing at, we have to go home
today and now we are going to be late.'

Thanks, Mum, for your concern.

The Tub was taken home at the end of each summer
and moored on the local river, tied to a tree. The
river, not a grand affair but wide enough for me to

row upstream and down as far as the weir, exploring the habitat. Much excitement in the spring and early summer watching many moorhens, even a swan nesting. I loved messing about on the river, loved it all.

The accident – Our rescue at sea wasn't the only excitement that day. Towing the caravan home, on a bend in the road in a little village – Stourpaine – we met a coach coming towards us in the middle of the road. The coach carried on blithely without incident, whereas we crashed into the nearside wall. Perhaps my mother was driving a little faster than she should, to make up for the time lost caused by our boating incident. I decided not to say, 'Well, Mum, we're definitely going to be late home now.'

At the time of the accident, I was on the back seat cradling a litter of puppies. With the impact, these were thrown to the floor of the car. They all survived, as I did, albeit with a banged head. Seatbelts in private cars were yet to be introduced.

Lynmouth – On an early caravan holiday in Swanage, we heard on the wireless about the Lynmouth disaster on the night of 15th August 1952. It had been raining heavily in Swanage, but nothing like the 23cm (9ins) of torrential rain that fell on Exmoor which cascaded in a raging torrent down the valley, engulfing Lynmouth. Over 100 buildings, comprising houses, shops and hotels were destroyed or severely damaged, and 38 cars washed into the sea. 34 people were killed or drowned on that fateful night.

The Lake District

One year, for a change, we holidayed in the English Lake District, towing a relatively new small touring caravan which gave just enough sleeping space for Mum and Dad, us kids destined to sleep in the attached awning — designed, created and pains-takingly stitched together by my talented mother.

A long journey with no motorways to speed us on our way – apart from the Preston bypass. This was the first-ever stretch of UK motorway, just opened, originally named the M62, now part of the M6. We didn't know what to expect but the motorway was very quiet, the road almost to ourselves. Dad remarked:

'I hope we see a sports car overtaking us, doing 100mph!'

We didn't. The M6 is very different today and it is unlikely any car travelling at 100mph would be spotted, not just because it is now illegal but due to the volume of traffic on the crowded motorway.

To break the journey, we spent a night on a caravan site close to Blackpool. That evening we drove into town for a fish supper and surprises – including the sound of voices, speaking in an unusual dialect, nothing like I was accustomed to in Wilshire. I'd not heard a northern accent before. In my ignorance, I turned to my father and commented:

'They talk a bit strange up here, Dad.'

That earned me another 'stupid boy' withering look, but with a generous half-smile.

Then more surprises, including the wide selection of chip shops to choose from – and I was astonished by the number and size of amusement arcades along the Golden Mile. The couple of chippies and amusements arcades in Swanage were nothing compared with the vast array on show in Blackpool. I had been leading a sheltered childhood.

In my excitement, I was not looking where I was walking, amazed by it all, which resulted in me slipping on a kerb and straining an ankle. This slightly immobilised me for the duration of the holiday.

We arrived at our chosen site at Borrowdale and anxious to start the holiday. But first there was the caravan to be levelled, the awning to be set up, water to be fetched and all the other paraphernalia involved. Finally, we were settled in and 'good to go.'

We explored extensively the lakes and valleys, by car and on foot. Despite my swelling ankle, I was fit enough to join Dad for some memorable Lakeland walks, including Crinkle Crags and

139

Catbells. Additionally, I experienced my first and only attempt at fishing – on Derwentwater, an eel being the total of my efforts.

I did not know it then, but this was to be my last trip away with my parents – all the more reason to be thankful for such a memorable holiday.

10

BEYOND HOME

News of the World

No, not the discredited and defunct Sunday rag, but my coverage of other aspects of living in the 1950s and news stories from the era. Many events passed by without me being aware, but some are well remembered, helped by listening to our parents or to the news on our old 'steam' radio.

The decade was a life generally full of community spirit, at times with a certain civil formality, but of goodness, virtue and Christian values. Christianity was by far the dominant religion, with church attendance considerably more evident than today.

All this was well before the permissive society of the Sixties and the later development of terrorism, which has become so much a threat to our way of life today. The illegal drug scene was in an early stage.

The arrival of the 1950s marked five years since the end of World War II, nonetheless life still very much continued as one of post-war austerity 'make do and mend'. Wages were low. Dresses were often homemade and it was not unknown for badly worn sheets to be cut in half with the outside edges sown together. And socks – who darns socks nowadays?

Computer World

A short section. Young people today are reminded that during the 1950s, indeed well beyond, we lived without mobile phones, social media, Google, Amazon and the rest. Some might find it hard to understand how we coped. But cope we did, in particular without the distraction of social media and the resultant pressure from which some young people now suffer. There is, of course, no going back from a now highly computerised world and all that that entails, both good and bad.

The Festival of Britain

This was held in 1951 on the South Bank of the Thames. I missed out on visiting the spectacle although Dad did buy me the commemorative stamp set: not quite the same thing. I was fairly pleased with the stamps but would much rather

142

have gone to the show. But later Dad did take me to London to visit Madame Tussauds (the apostrophe was removed in 2007). To my regret, he wouldn't let me into the 'Chamber of Horrors' and now I will never witness the spectacle as the chamber closed on 11th April 2016.

One main intention of the Festival was to give a feeling that Britain was recovering from the War, and it did indeed instil the stirrings of a 'feel -good' factor.

Long live the Queen

On the 6th February 1952, King George VI died from a lung condition; it was the fags wot did it for him. The nation plunged into mourning. Princess Elizabeth, now Queen Elizabeth II, was in Kenya when the news broke: she made a rapid return to London.

Her much-anticipated Coronation took place on 2nd June 1953. It rained all day. This turned out not to be a bad omen as, at the time of writing, our good Queen is still very much with us, despite the trials and tribulations caused by certain members of her family.

To watch the Coronation, all our family, and extended family, gathered around the minuscule black and white TV set. To pass the time for the younger members of the family, a game of

Monopoly was arranged. This took an age to play, even longer than the game usually takes, not just due to the number of players taking part: the game regularly stopped to watch the televised proceedings. Between my turns to play I drifted aimlessly around the house, thoroughly bored.

At other family leisure times, games included Snakes and Ladders which I found more satisfying. My bar was set pretty low.

Also in 1953, New Zealander Sir Edmund Hillary and Sherpa Tensing Norgay conquered Mount Everest. The aim was to achieve this before the Coronation – which they did with just four days to spare. The mountain has been climbed many times since and continues to be regularly scaled, but you can't beat being the first.

A tour by the Queen of the Commonwealth in late 1953 created much excitement at school. The tour included two days in Fiji. We were told that when in that country she would be required to 'burp' after eating, a sign of good manners to show she enjoyed the meal, apparently; great hilarity all round in class.

In December that year, the Queen made her first Christmas broadcast, by radio, to round off an eventful year for her. The annual message has been televised since 1957.

Teds, beehives and coffee

The later 1950s: the era of teddy boys, all uniformly adorned with sideburns, lashings of Brylcreem on their hair, drainpipe trousers, winkle-picker shoes, possibly a flick knife and/or knuckle-duster in their pocket. And beehives for the girls, a popular hairstyle for the young and not so young ladies in the Fifties. I am not an expert on the subject but I believe the beehive effect was created by severe backcombing the hair; surely not good for the health of the hair.

The 'Teds', as they were commonly known, and the beehive-clad girls, met in so-called Expresso coffee bars. I mentioned these earlier and that my parents would not allow me to enter therein, such establishments considered by them to be dens of vice and iniquity. (Sounded ok to me). From all accounts, and I have to be guided by other reports here, espresso was not actually the product on sale. Apparently, it bore little resemblance to proper barista-served coffee from a genuine Gaggia coffee machine, more like weak powdered instant – or 'Camp' perhaps?

Camp coffee – there was always an old bottle of this chicory and coffee essence liquid (still available today) in our food cupboard. Mum said it was dreadful stuff but being frugal, couldn't bring herself to throw the bottle away.

Eating out

Eating out in a restaurant was a rare event until the 1960s (and not a regular occurrence even then) and it would need to be a special occasion to justify the cost for financially hard-pressed families. The height of high living for us was fish and chips from the local chippy. There were pubs, of course, although not the gastro pubs seen today.

On occasions, with baby sitters hard to come by, our parents took us to their local, not for a meal but just a drink – a pint for Dad and a sherry (large) for Mum. We three kids were left in the car with a packet of crisps each, a practise they started way back during the Bridport and West Bay holiday. If Dad was feeling particularly generous, we might be the happy recipients of a large bottle of pop to share.

Somewhere to live

The Second World War caused the loss of much family accommodation. Prefabs (prefabricated) homes were built in considerable numbers as short-term temporary accommodation and intended to be in use for a maximum of ten years. They could be very comfortable to live in, were it not for the struggle to keep the home warm. Energy efficient they were not. In the event, prefabs lasted much longer than ten years. A large estate in Melksham was still there when I left primary school in 1956, and for several years after that.

In the 1960s, a platonic girlfriend lived in a prefab in Bristol, near Frenchay Hospital (since closed). I spent many a happy and cosy evening with her and her family, they were great fun to be with. They loved where they lived and dreaded when the day would arrive for them to be re-housed.

In time, families were rehoused with tears from those who had become very attached to their temporary homes. Today, there is some talk of reintroducing the concept of prefabricated homes to relieve the current housing crisis. If this goes ahead, the modern prefab will be built to a much higher standard and, most importantly, will be highly energy efficient.

The Media

Newspapers, radio and television news included much coverage on the government of the day – as now – and politicians came in for a fair amount of stick – as now.

One quiet evening at home in a moment of rare clarity of thought, I felt a selection of celebrities and industry leaders might do a better job running the country than the current lot. I compiled a list of my favoured cabinet and, with tongue in cheek, posted it to the Daily Express, my parents' choice of newspaper at the time. I received a telegram from the paper, 'May we publish?'. No doubt I had not addressed my scribbled correspondence correctly.

With Dad's help, I replied with a hurried telegram in the affirmative. The letter was not published but recently I have enjoyed some success with letters appearing in national newspapers and periodicals. Unsurprisingly, this has not led to a flurry of offers to be a newspaper columnist.

11

FURTHER AFIELD

Australia

Australia is a member of the Commonwealth, although currently there is an increasingly republican attitude in the country.

From the end of the Second World War until 1972, British citizens were encouraged to consider emigration to Australia. A passage could be purchased for just £10 a head (the '£10 Pom Scheme') with the true cost of the dramatically subsidised voyage shared between the UK and Australian governments. This offer was much talked about at school as the publicity for the scheme was compelling. Many of us tried to persuade our parents to take up the offer: we all failed. But well over one million British subjects did take advantage of the subsidy to start a new life on the far side of the world.

Racism

At school we were aware of the abhorrent apartheid in South Africa. I was more aware than most as my paternal grandmother lived in the country for some years. On returning to the UK she showed me photographic evidence of apartheid, examples including signs at public toilets, swimming pools, beaches and on park benches: 'Whites Only'. Shops displayed signs like 'We cater for whites only.'

Apartheid came to a thankful end in 1994 after protracted negotiations, but equality was still not achieved. On my visit to the country in 2005, the white minority still held most of the senior, managerial and other well-paid jobs, with the native population confined to manual work.

Racist attitudes were not confined to South Africa. In the UK, boarding houses displayed signs such as 'No blacks, Irish or dogs', particularly in Liverpool, but also in London and other cities. We have come a long way since then but regretfully evidence of racism, anti-Semitism and general intolerance to others is still much in evidence today.

The Cold War

We were enlightened that during the 1950s and beyond, the world was living through the 'Cold War' which involved much posturing between the USSR (Union of Soviet Socialist Republics) and the West. This state of affairs was called the Cold War as verbal aggression was maintained without the use of warfare. This is a simplistic two-sentence summary on a subject about which many books have been written.

Both sides continued their arms race to increase their conventional armoury and, in addition, their stock of nuclear weapons (the 'nuclear deterrent'). On the 3rd of October 1952, Britain carried out her first nuclear test in Western Australia. Then on 17th October 1956, the first nuclear power station opened at Calder Hall, 10 miles south of Whitehaven (decommissioned in 2003).

On the 15th May 1957 Britain's first hydrogen bomb test was carried out on Christmas Island in the Indian Ocean. This resulted in widescale opposition at home and abroad and led to the formation of the Campaign for Nuclear Disarmament (CND) in 1958.

Later came the Cuba Crisis with the world on the brink of nuclear war. This took place in the 1960s and therefore beyond the scope of this book, as was

Chernobyl in 1986, which in part brought about the collapse of the USSR at the end of 1991, and the fall of the Berlin Wall.

This led to hopes being raised that Russia would develop into a true democracy. Some hopes. This has not materialised with, to date, little apparent change in the behaviour of the current Russian leadership.

The Suez Crisis

In 1956, President Nasser of Egypt nationalised the Suez Canal, a British/French jointly-owned enterprise. There was a complex political run-up to the canal being seized by Nasser, and economic repercussions thereafter, including petrol rationing as I touched on earlier. Prime Minister Sir Anthony Eden was forced to resign, although this was partly due to his poor health.

This sorry saga marked a further decline in Britain as a once major world power.

The Outlook

Thankfully for the economy, petrol rationing did not last long and, arguably, by the later 1950s life was beginning to look a little brighter. In January 1957 Harold Macmillan was elected leader of the

Conservative Party and as Prime Minister, made his 'You've never had it so good' speech, urging wage restraint at a time of increasing inflation.

This was not popular with other political persuasions who strongly disagreed with him, although my brother, who later tried his hand at politics, displayed a large poster containing Macmillan's political message on his bedroom wall.

But politics was not Tony's only interest – alongside this poster he displayed, equally prominently and equally large, a poster produced by Heineken with *their* catchphrase: 'Refreshes the parts other beers cannot reach.' This marketing slogan has been around for a very long time.

The Space Race

Much excitement at school at the thought of man-made satellites circling the globe. The USA and USSR were racing to be the first to achieve this goal. Really, there was no contest as the Russians were going to win and win they did, with the launch of 'Sputnik 1' on 4th October 1957, a major coup for them in the ongoing Cold War. The satellite survived for three months before re-entering the earths' atmosphere.

The first attempt by the United States at launching a satellite – on 6th December 1957 –resulted in an ignominious explosion, but Explorer 1 was launched successfully on 31st January 1958.

12

ALL CHANGE

My reflections within this book cover the 1950s, but as my life was to experience a significant transformation at the end of 1961, I am including observations on my final two years living in Wiltshire.

A Bombshell

As I said earlier, Dad managed a tobacco factory in Devizes – Anstie & Co –– where he worked so hard for his employers. Perhaps in recognition of his labours, in 1960 the board offered him a directorship. Mum was delighted.

'What pay rise will you get, John?', she asked excitedly.

'No, no pay rise, I look upon it as an honour, I am very pleased they think well of me.'

Mum, always somewhat mercenary, was most unhappy but in this case I think she had a valid point. Dad was a mild and modest man, never one to push himself forward.

In the event it made little difference as on the first of March 1961 a bombshell hit us. Anstie's was to be bought out by the Bristol-based Churchman's Tobacco Company, their business plan being to close Anstie's and amalgamate manufacturing within their Bristol operations. All 100 staff on the shop floor at Anstie's were to lose their jobs. My father was offered a senior clerical position at the company's Redcliffe offices – if prepared to move to Bristol. At his age, facing little likelihood of obtaining alternative employment in Wiltshire, he decided to take the job. We were to move to Bristol.

My parents did first look at a property in Chippenham, not that far from Bristol, nor far from Devizes where they enjoyed a small social circle. In retrospect, I am glad that didn't happen. There was probably little of interest for me in Chippenham, although I am sure the good people of that fine town are very happy living there. I didn't know it yet, but Bristol was going to suit me just fine. My parents moved to Bristol in the summer of 1961, but I wasn't ready to join them just yet.

A Welsh adventure

I sat my GCE examinations in June that year but feared I had not done well: the school agreed I could stay on for another term to take resits in December.

I was in no hurry to hear the results that summer, knowing they would not be good, so as they were about to be released I embarked on a holiday in Wales with David. I cycled to Trowbridge to link up with him. From there we set off on our adventure, reaching the Aust ferry that evening. We crossed the River Severn then cycled through the Welsh countryside all night, and the following day, until we collapsed from exhaustion at 5.00pm.

We slept in a field on the outskirts of Llandovery for an hour, just enough to give us the energy to continue our journey to our destination at Pumpsaint, arriving there at 8.00 pm after a total journey of 120 miles. We set up camp with a small tent and slept soundly that night for 12 hours or more.

Or camp was at the site of the Roman Dolaucothi gold mines, abandoned now, but Welsh gold was mined there spasmodically since Roman times. The mines finally closed in 1936. We spent our few days there exploring the disused mines, no doubt a dangerous pastime but great fun. Safer now, but less exciting, as the mines are managed by the National Trust. With hammer and chisel we each excavated small chunks of granite containing the vaguest seams of gold. I still have mine.

In the evenings we introduced ourselves to the mysteries and delights of Welsh beer and cider, the local publican appearing unconcerned with our youthful appearance. One evening the locals in the bar warned us that the gold mines were haunted by a Roman centurion. Sometimes he could be heard torturing the wretched slaves working in the mines. Nonsense, surely!

We returned to our tent that night well inebriated and soon fell asleep, only to be awakened later by hideous noises appearing to be emanating from the mine adjacent to us. We looked at each other in horror. What was that? A severely frightening experience and it took a while before we realised we had been set up by our 'friends' in the pub.

After a glorious few days, we cycled home to face our results. Surprisingly, I passed all my exams, albeit with very modest marks. But by this time the decision had been taken that I would stay on at school and be boarded for this extra term by David's kind parents.

My final term

At the start of my final term in September 1961, the headmaster told me I couldn't just 'swan around' (or whatever was the expression of the day). He enrolled me in an 'A' level course in maths, both pure and applied, and French. Maths was my strongest subject at GCE level but this advanced course left me struggling, soon sinking fast, not helped by my frame of mind. My heart was elsewhere. To help with my French, I was advised to enrol for evening classes, so I did. David signed up too. We didn't take the course too seriously and now being 16-years-old, should really have behaved responsibly. David lighting matches under our college desk did not endear us to the lecturer – a master from school, no less.

During the term I lived in Bristol with my parents at weekends, then cycled to Trowbridge (24 miles distant) early on Monday mornings in time for school at 9.00am., the journey being reversed on Friday afternoons. This arrangement was tiring but worked for a few weeks until I purchased a motor scooter – the first of many – a 125cc Capri, from Whalley's on Cheltenham Road in Bristol; definitely a step in the right direction.

As I spent only the one term in the sixth form, I never made the grade as a school prefect but did rise to the dizzy height of dinner monitor. I was even allowed to hand out 'lines' to misbehaving younger boys, though no permission to dole out physical punishment. That was reserved for the pleasure of others. I remember that quote, allegedly spoken by schoolmasters:

'This will hurt me more than you.'

I don't think so. Watching others being punished, I am sure I saw a glint in the eye of more than one master.

During this final term I attended two interviews with Lloyds Bank, first in Bristol then London – my first trip to the capital on my own and my first experience of navigating the underground system.

After an agonising wait, I was offered a job, to start on 8th January 1962 at the Totterdown branch in Bristol. The branch is long gone, now a successful café and bar, a much more appealing use of the premises.

13

MOVING ON

In conclusion, I look back on my school days with mixed emotions. I remember some glorious times, happy and carefree, but also a darker side when I was just unhappy and down at heart, not helped by restrictions in activities caused by my poor eyesight. Some say your school days are the happiest days of your life. That might be the case for some but in all truth, not for me.

Towards the end of my final year I dreaded how I would cope living in the big city permanently. I was just a country boy at heart, sad to be leaving friendships behind. As it turned out, I had no need to worry. My life was to become so different from my school days – my first full-time job, the attractions of a big city, and more. Much more.

Further recollections are continued in my book, *'Young Love in Sixties Bristol'*.

About the Author

Chris Walker was born in Bristol in 1945 on the day before VE day. Just ten months after the end of the war, his family moved out of Bristol and settled for rural life in Wiltshire. He moved back to Bristol in 1962, joining a bank. He worked in various locations in the city, then London, and one brief spell in New York.

Now retired, he lives in Farnham, Surrey. He is married with three daughters and six grandchildren.

This is his second publication.

Printed in Great Britain
by Amazon